SECOND EDITION

HOW TO HANDLE

SECOND EDITION

HOW TO HANDLE

DIFFICULT
PARENTS

Proven Solutions for Teachers

Suzanne Capek Tingley

PRUFROCK PRESS INC.
WACO, TEXAS

Library of Congress Cataloging-in-Publication Data

Tingley, Suzanne Capek.
  How to handle difficult parents : proven solutions for teachers / by Suzanne Capek Tingley. -- 2nd ed.
      p. cm.
  Includes bibliographical references.
  ISBN 978-1-59363-958-7 (pbk.)
  1. Parent-teacher relationships--Handbooks, manuals, etc. 2. Aggressiveness--Prevention--Handbooks,
manuals, etc. 3. Communication in education--Handbooks, manuals, etc. I. Title.
  LC226.6.T56 2012
  371.103--dc23
                        2012011467

Prufrock Press Inc.
P.O. Box 8813
Waco, TX 76714-8813
Phone: (800) 998-2208
Fax: (800) 240-0333
http://www.prufrock.com

Table of Contents

Chapter 1
Dealing With Parents 101

Despite what some people may think, not everyone can be a teacher. Teaching is a challenging but rewarding career, one that actually makes a difference in people's lives. But it takes skill, commitment, and courage.

People become teachers because they love working with kids. They have spent 4 or more years becoming experts in one or more content areas: reading, math, physical education, music, English, science, special education, foreign language, or social studies. They have learned how to plan a lesson, create valid tests, diversify instruction, and run inclusive classrooms. They have practiced effective teaching strategies and classroom management techniques during their student teaching or internship experiences. In short, they arrive at their first teaching jobs eager to embrace the challenges of the profession.

If they are lucky, they will be among the 200,000 new teachers hired each fall across the nation. They will enter the field with high expectations and a willingness to work hard to improve their skills.

In 2 years, 10% of them will quit.

In 3 years, about 40% will quit.

By the end of 5 years, about 50%—fully half of those new, optimistic teachers who have spent so much time, money, and effort to prepare themselves for their careers—will have left the profession, according to studies conducted by the National Bureau of Statistics and the National Education Association in 2006 (see National Education Association, 2010).

Some new teachers who leave find student discipline overwhelming. Others point to a lack of administrative support. But one of the main reasons for leaving the profession, according to the Center for Strengthening the Teaching Profession (Plecki, Elfers, Loeb, Zahir, & Knapp, 2005), is this: Teachers are unprepared to work with difficult parents.

TEACHERS ARE UNPREPARED TO WORK WITH DIFFICULT PARENTS

Despite all of their training, new teachers often lack the skills needed to handle the demands of some of today's parents.

There's Justin's mother, for example, who thinks that it's okay for her son to stick mozzarella sticks up his nose during lunch ("He's such a character!").

There's Samantha's stepdad, who says it's the teacher's fault that Samantha cheated on her social studies test ("Why weren't you watching her more closely?").

Keisha's mother did her daughter's science project for her and then complained that the work only got a B ("Do you have any idea how much time this took?").

Bradley's father threatened to have the teacher fired if she didn't change his son's math grade ("It will be your fault if he doesn't get into his first-choice college!").

And Lee's mother's boyfriend says Lee doesn't deserve detention because fighting is what boys do ("I'm the one who taught him to fight!").

Dealing with difficult parents isn't the only reason that teachers abandon the profession, but the stress of doing so remains one of the top reasons teachers cite for leaving the ranks.

TEACHERS NEED TO LEARN PARENT MANAGEMENT SKILLS

Teachers who remain in the classroom discover that, in addition to classroom management skills, they must develop parent management skills if they want to be successful. Without such skills, an adversarial relationship between a teacher and a parent can take its toll.

For example, when teachers know that a child's parent stands ready to challenge them at every turn, they can become reluctant to confront inappropriate student behavior or lack of effort. When they know that a dreaded "helicopter mom" is always hovering nearby, ready to swoop in at a moment's notice to protect her child, teachers may feel that it's not worth the personal stress to stand up for what they know is in the child's best interest. When they know that a student's father will go directly to the principal if he's unhappy with his child's grade, they begin to feel perpetually defensive. In short, dealing with difficult parents can have a demoralizing effect on the individual teacher and even on the school as a whole, particularly if teachers feel that they have to fend for themselves without administrative support or a comprehensive school policy for working with parents.

Let me hasten to point out that I am not talking about all parents. Most parents are supportive, helpful, and realistic. They volunteer as band

> *Any teacher can develop an array of strategies that will prove successful a great deal of the time.*

boosters and help with bake sales. They attend their kid's performances and vote for the school budget. They take an interest in their child's progress, work with teachers as partners, and communicate with them respectfully and civilly. Although they sometimes disagree with the school's position, it is their right to do so. (It's fine for parents to disagree. It's not fine for them to be disagreeable.)

Let me also agree that, yes, difficult teachers exist in every school system, creating their own set of problems. However, even the best and most reasonable teachers around the country report that a growing number of parents make excuses for their children, refuse to allow them to take any responsibility, and believe that every wish their child makes should be granted. Teachers who refuse to accept excuses, insist on student responsibility, and aren't afraid of saying no are bound to find themselves in eventual conflict with parents who make unreasonable demands and criticize or even threaten their children's teachers when those demands aren't met.

ALL TEACHERS CAN LEARN TO HANDLE PARENTS MORE EFFECTIVELY

What can a teacher do when faced with a problem parent? No single strategy will work for all situations. However, any teacher can develop an array of strategies that will prove successful a great deal of the time.

In the following chapters, you'll find plenty of effective techniques, including what to say and what not to say, and how they can be used in specific situations. You will find them helpful whether you're a new teacher or a veteran.

4

Chapter 2
A Short and Subjective History of Parents

THE ANCIENTS

In 1900, Mark Twain, in an address to the Public Education Association, observed that, "Out of the public school grows the greatness of a nation." The waves of immigrants to the United States in the first quarter of the 20th century resulted in legislation making public school attendance compulsory for children for the first time. Compulsory education not only "Americanized" the younger generation, but it also kept them out of the factories where children had previously competed with adults for jobs.

During those years and for many years that followed, parents went to work and their children went to school, the children often moving well beyond their parents in terms of formal education. Few parents questioned how the school was run or whether their children were being taught well or treated fairly. They believed school was their children's responsibility, just as work was theirs.

When my brother, sister, and I were children in the 1950s and 1960s, for example, our parents did not contact our teachers if we didn't like an assignment. They did not call the principal to complain if we got detention.

They did not believe that we never lied. They did not care if we were bored in school, and they did not accept being bored as an excuse for poor grades. They did not believe that children had "personality conflicts" with teachers because children's personalities had little standing in their book. They did not tell us that we should respect teachers only if they respected us. They were wise enough to know that our version of what happened at school that day was just that—our version. They did not know what our math homework was, and they didn't care. Whatever it was, they expected us to do it. In some ways, we had a freedom that today's children can't even imagine.

Our parents' disinterest in the details of school did not mean they were bad parents. In fact, they were great parents. They were very clear, however, about their expectations for us in terms of school. Like the parents in every other family we knew, their expectation was this: "If you get in trouble at school, that's nothing compared to what will happen when you get home."

I don't want to give the impression that my parents didn't care about us or about our education. They did. They made sure we reported to school every single day unless we were running a fever, had spots, or were throwing up. They knew when report cards were issued, they reviewed them, and then they signed them. They went to all of our concerts, plays, and awards programs. (The only things they didn't attend were our summer baseball or softball league games. Watching us do the same thing we did in the middle of our street, except on a field where first base was a sack instead of the sewer cover, was not a reason to take off work. In truth, the only parents who ever watched us play ball in the summer were dads who were out of work for one reason or another.)

They were just busy—busy attending to their responsibilities of working hard, raising a family, and paying the bills. We were expected to attend to our responsibilities—going to school every day, staying out of trouble, and paying attention. In a sense, they had their jobs and we had ours.

We did not feel deprived.

Kids who had formerly been described as "lazy" (a word we teachers were now forbidden to use) were now "bored."

THINGS START TO CHANGE

I became a teacher myself in the late 1970s, and it seemed to me that parents of that era were, for the most part, similar to my parents. They still expected their kids to do their job while they did theirs. They were still suspicious of their children's renditions of what happened in school that day, and they still expected their children to behave. Here's a typical conversation from that era:

Teacher: Tommy swore in class today.

Mr. Smith: I'm sorry. We'll take care of it at home.

Teacher: He's going to need to serve a detention.

Mr. Smith: That's fine with us.

Here's another example:

Teacher: If Madeline can stay after school on Thursdays, I can help her with spelling.

Mrs. Torres: She'll be there. You hear that, Madeline? Every Thursday.

However, by the early 1980s, I began to see a slight abdication of parental authority. Typical conversations of that era tended to sound more like this:

Teacher: Mrs. Jones, I'm having a little trouble getting Jack to do his homework.

Mrs. Jones: If you can't make him do it, what do you expect me to do?

Or:

Teacher: Mr. Fazio, Jennifer really needs to stay after school for extra help.

Mr. Fazio: Well, she's a lot like me—doesn't like to be told what to do.

Around this time we began to hear about "bored" children. Kids who had formerly been described as "lazy" (a word we teachers were now forbidden to use) were now "bored." Reading bored them. Math bored them. Writing bored them. Homework especially bored them. The reason for all this boredom? These kids were *way* smarter than the other kids, according to their parents.

Of course, these students typically didn't demonstrate their boredom by staring out the window, doodling, or coming up with creative solutions for problems. Instead, they did no work at all or disrupted the class. This, according to their parents, was because they weren't being sufficiently challenged.

No one I knew when I was a kid ever admitted to being bored. I learned early in life never to say to my mother, "There's nothing to do around here," because she would quickly find something for me to do: vacuum, pick beans, take out the garbage, clean the garage. It never would have occurred to her (or to me) that it was her job to entertain me if I was bored.

However, as a teacher, I began to feel that was exactly what some parents expected me to do with their kids—entertain them. If their children weren't doing anything in class, it wasn't because they were lazy or because they had legitimate issues like learning disabilities. It was because they were so smart that the work in class was beneath them. The "challenge" they needed was really mine: to motivate them or perhaps . . . to entertain them.

By this point, I had kids of my own. Watching *Sesame Street* with them, I began to see how they could grow up believing that all learning could be fun. Number facts should be set to music, and letters could sing and dance!

Well, I wanted learning to be fun, too, but I knew that was not always possible. Although my 1980s hairstyle made me look like one, I was not a Muppet.

THE DECADE ENDS

At the beginning of the 1990s, I began to see a big difference in the attitude of some parents toward schools, teachers, and their own kids. By then, I had become the principal of a middle school/high school, and many conversations with parents began to sound like this:

Principal: Mr. Yung, Jeremy was in a fight this afternoon, and I am going to have to suspend him for a day.

Mr. Yung: What about the other kid? He started it! He better be getting 2 days!

Or:

Principal: Mrs. Golden, Ann was disrespectful to her physical education teacher this afternoon.

Mrs. Golden: How was she disrespectful?

Principal: She told the teacher that she wasn't going to do any f-ing push-ups.

Mrs. Golden: So what did her teacher do to provoke her?

Unfortunately, this trend continued over the next years, headed steadily, in my opinion, downhill. Today when a student has a problem at school, there's a much greater chance that the parents will not accept the consequences of their child's behavior without argument.

When a child gets in trouble today, conversations are more likely to sound like the one I had not long ago over an incident involving a middle schooler:

Principal: Mike, whatever made you think that mooning the other team from the bus was a good idea?

Mike: (*shrugging his shoulders*) I dunno.

As a middle schooler, Mike probably *didn't* know. (It's a given that middle schoolers sometimes don't think before they act.) But when told that Mike was being suspended for a few days to ponder the question, his father gave this response:

Mike's dad: You're overreacting. Didn't you ever do something like that?

I wondered briefly what there is about me that would make Mike's dad think that I too mooned an opposing team when I was 13. The fact that I was still alive should have convinced him that I would never have done that!

9

So here's what I said to him:

Principal: Oh, for Pete's sake. Gimme a break. No wonder your kid thinks mooning someone is okay.

I didn't say that, of course. I *thought* it, though. Here's what I really said:

Principal: Mike may return to school in 3 days.

There have always been demanding parents. However, demanding parents of earlier times were more likely to demand that their *kids* do what they wanted them to do, not the *teachers*.

What best describes parents today? In my opinion, it is a belief that their kids should have anything their little hearts desire.

THE MODERNS

What best describes parents today? In my opinion, it is a belief that their kids should have anything their little hearts desire. Unfortunately, schools may have contributed to this notion. That wasn't the intent, of course, but the result of a good idea run amok.

Starting in schools in the early 1990s, and continuing into this century, was a belief in the importance of self-esteem. It was deemed more important than reading and math, more important than discipline, more important than problem solving, more important than just about anything. At its worst, though no one actually said so, it took the form of, "Well, if little Mikey can't read, at least he can feel good about himself as an illiterate."

Competition became inherently bad because if someone were first, someone else would have to be last. The dodge balls were put in the closet, and instead we played cooperative games like grasping the edges of a silk parachute and watching the wind lift it up.

All too often, everyone got a ribbon just for participating. Perfect attendance awards were given out for near-perfect attendance as well (absent fewer than 15 times!). Ten kids in a class received the "Most Improved" award at the end of the year. "Inventive" spelling sometimes lasted far beyond elementary school and didn't need to be corrected before the written piece was displayed on the bulletin board. The "math minute" became the "math 6 minutes" so that no one would feel bad about not finishing the 10 problems required for a star.

Everyone was special in his or her own way. There were no "wrong" answers. Conversations often went something like this:

Teacher: How much is 6 times 8?

Student: 36?

Teacher: Good try! What else could it be?

Grades of A, B, and C on elementary report cards often changed to new, inoffensive letters that carried no baggage—like N (needs improvement), M (making progress), and S (sometimes gets it). Kids needed to "construct" meaning at their own pace, even if it meant drawing for most of the time instead of learning number facts.

All right, I'm exaggerating, but there was a tendency to believe that raising self-esteem required lowering our expectations. We began to believe that children should be rewarded not only for doing something good, but also for not doing something bad:

Teacher: Because no one hit anyone today, tomorrow we will have a popcorn party!

Raising a child's self-esteem also meant *asking* rather than *telling* children what we wanted them to do. Teachers needed to give children choices.

Old way: Class, get out your spelling books.

New way: Class, would you like to work on spelling now?

Or:

Old way: If you can't share, we'll put those toys away. And stop that pinching immediately, or you'll find yourself in the time-out chair!

New way: We need you to share those toys, okay? And no more pinching, all right?

Or:

Old way: Put the balls away now.

New way: We need to put the balls away now, okay? Is everybody ready to put the balls away? Okay, let's put them all away, all right?

Of course, children were smart enough to sense that putting the balls away or not was not a real choice like, "Do you want mustard on your hot dog?" or "Do you want to go swimming or go to the mall?" They knew instinctively that responding with a resounding "No!" to "Is everybody ready to put the balls away?" would simply result in more wheedling from the adult. Although they knew that playtime would eventually end, they also knew they didn't have to do what was asked the first time or maybe even the fifth or sixth time. They would be able to tell when the teacher actually meant what she said because then she would go back to the old way of giving directions:

Teacher: "Put those balls away NOW!"

SELF-ESTEEM ISN'T RAISED BY LOWERING EXPECTATIONS

All of this is not to say that self-esteem doesn't matter. It does. No one should have to be picked last in a gym class. There are dozens of ways of choosing up sides without making a kid feel like a loser before the game even gets started. And there are hundreds of ways, maybe thousands of ways, maybe millions of ways of helping kids grow, learn, and make good mistakes on their way to discovering how to make good decisions.

Our intentions were good, but we unwittingly bought into what turned out to be the myths of self-esteem. Here's one example of the myths:

Myth: Low self-esteem is the primary cause of low academic achievement.

Fact: It's the other way around.

In our eagerness to help kids feel good about themselves, we overlooked the one thing guaranteed to achieve that result: actual accomplishment. Even a kindergartner knows when he's done something really worthy of praise. In our rush to enhance self-esteem, we underestimated how important real accomplishment is to kids.

Kids want to do well, and they want to please. They want to know what the target is so they can try to hit it. They also want consistent adult guidance and direction as they learn how to do things. Here's another myth:

Myth: Self-esteem predicts success.

Fact: Self-control and the ability to delay rewards are the strongest predictors of success.

With the emphasis on self-esteem, teachers often soft-pedaled criticism and lowered their standards in a misguided attempt not to harm the child's delicate psyche. Kids discovered to their initial delight and later dismay that even their smallest efforts were rewarded. All of those trophies and certificates really didn't mean anything if everyone got them. (Have you ever noticed at elementary awards ceremonies where everyone gets a certificate of some kind that many kids leave their awards on the floor under their chairs when the ceremony is over?) So, being kids, they began to test the limits to see how far they had to go before an adult would actually step up to the plate.

Lowering expectations often meant adults responding quickly to find some kind of amusement if a child complained about being bored. Instead of insisting that children behave and control themselves, adults looked for reasons to excuse bad behavior—the child was overly tired, had consumed too many sweets, it was too hot outside, or she didn't get

> *Even a kindergartner knows when he's done something really worthy of praise.*

to wear her favorite shirt. Of course, some of these issues can contribute to poor behavior, but after a certain age—3 or 4 maybe—kids shouldn't automatically get a pass because of them. Sometimes kids act out because they want to! Because they're kids! Which brings us to one more myth:

Myth: Low self-esteem causes aggressive behavior.

Fact: Bullies and other aggressors have been shown to have higher than average self-esteem.

Numerous studies have shown that bullies are bullies because they feel they are stronger than those they bully and that they can do it with impunity. Teachers often console the victim of a bully by saying, "You know, he just doesn't feel very good about himself, and he's taking it out on you." I have to admit I said that myself as a teacher, and it wasn't much of an intervention or a consolation. (Happily, we're taking a much different and assertive approach to bullying these days.)

For a period, schools abandoned high standards for behavior and academics in the hopes of developing happy children. It didn't work.

PARENTS JOIN THE SELF-ESTEEM MOVEMENT

Taking their lead from school, parents also began to believe that a child's self-esteem could be damaged easily if any of his or her actions or ideas met with disapproval. For far too many parents, the word "no" became both rare and negotiable.

Parents momentarily forgot who was in charge:

Mom: (*to her 5-year-old*) Mommy's tired of the escalator. Aren't you tired of the escalator? Okay, one more time. But then we need to go home, okay? Well, just one more time after that. Then that's it, okay?

Parents forgot that actions speak louder than words:

Parent: Johnny, don't make me come over there. Johnny, I mean it. Don't make me come over there. Stop that now. I don't want to have to come over there. You hear me? I mean it. Don't make me come over there.

For far too many parents, the word "no" became both rare and negotiable.

14

Parents forgot that they were older and more experienced than their kids:

Dad: (*to his 9-year old*) How many times do I have to tell you not to pee on the rhododendrons? Look! They're all dead. I've told you a dozen times. How long are you going to keep doing that?!

And some parents seemed to have momentarily lost their minds:

Mom: (*to her toddler, at the grocery store*) I know you're angry, and you can hit Mommy, but not too hard.

At a restaurant one morning, a little boy wearing a beanie with a propeller attached was allowed to scream and race around the restaurant, annoying other patrons while his father smiled indulgently. When the family finally left, one older diner said loudly, "The wrong person is wearing the beanie in that family."

The result of the self-esteem movement was that kids' self-esteem stayed the same but adults' self-esteem plummeted. Kids began to believe that if nothing was actually required of them, they must be entitled to do whatever they wanted. For a while there it wasn't pretty.

Eventually, however, most teachers and parents got tired of asking kids a dozen times to do what they were supposed to do. When many of them came to their senses, they began to remember that when a child misbehaves, it doesn't necessarily signal a lack of confidence, but instead a lack of discipline. Or maybe a lack of clear expectations on the part of the adult. Or maybe (gasp!) a lack of consequences.

THE PENDULUM SWINGS

Of course, keeping with education tradition, schools didn't just recognize the error of their ways. They overcompensated. The pendulum swung w-a-a-a-ay to the other side. Today, instead of making excuses and indulging kids' errors in judgment, we have embraced the equally ridiculous idea of "zero tolerance." Today the operative concept in education isn't self-esteem, but *assessment*—a test for everything.

And not long ago kids got ribbons just for running around the soccer field in the summer or remembering their lunch money for a week or learning their five weekly vocabulary words. Now we test them in every class, at every level, in every subject. Kids can forget about ribbons for participation. Either they can pass the test or they can't.

What happens to a child's self-esteem when a low test score lands her in third grade for a second time? Or when a 10-year-old with the ability of a preschooler is forced, because the state mandates it, to sit for a 2-hour test? Or when a high school student with superior computer programming skills can't pass the required foreign language test? Self-esteem is no longer the major concern. Test scores are. No Child Left Untested.

As for zero tolerance, of course no child should bring a weapon to school, and the consequences must be serious. But is a spork a weapon? Are toy soldiers with plastic guns a weapon? And I agree with a zero tolerance for drugs in school, but aspirin?

Wouldn't a little thoughtful moderation be nice for a change?

High-stakes testing makes parents nervous for their children, and rightfully so. All parents want their children to be successful, and not just so Dad's car can sport a bumper sticker proclaiming, "My child is on the Supreme Deluxe Honor Roll," as if his kid were some kind of taco. Parents want their children to have friends, to get good grades, and to like school. It may not always seem that way to the teacher, but parents really do want their children to have a positive attitude toward teachers and toward learning.

THERE ARE VARIABLES IN EDUCATION, AND THERE ARE CONSTANTS

One thing that hasn't changed in all of the history of parents is that kids do better when there is mutual support and respect between home and school. Hot-button issues in education come and go, but a strong connection between home and school remains one of the most reliable indicators of a child's potential for success. In developing strategies to work with parents, it is crucial that teachers never forget this important idea—that when teachers and parents work together, the child benefits.

> *When teachers and parents work together, the child benefits.*

Chapter 3
The Acorn May Not Fall Far From the Oak

After school has been in session for a few weeks, most teachers have identified some concerns they have about some of their students. Of course, a natural course of action is to meet with parents to see if they can share any insight into working with their child. But what if, 5 minutes into a parent-teacher conference, you find yourself with a clarity you didn't expect?

Imagine the following conversation, for example:

Teacher: Heidi is a smart girl, but when I ask her to stop talking, she gives me attitude.

Parent: (*big sigh*) Like what?

Teacher: She's disrespectful.
Parent: How is she disrespectful?
Teacher: The expression on her face and her tone of voice.
Parent: (*rolling her eyes*) Oh, big deal.

Or:

Teacher: Tim needs to clean up his language.
Parent: Sh-t, he's just a kid.

Or:

Parent: This is the third time this year you've sent Bart home with head lice.
School Nurse: He can't be in school with nits.
Parent: He looked pretty good this morning.
School Nurse: Did you check his head?
Parent: No, but he looked in the mirror and said they were gone.

Or:

Teacher: The problem is that when I try to correct Annie's behavior, she insists that she's not doing anything wrong.
Parent: Maybe she isn't.
Teacher: I've watched her break another student's crayons and then deny doing it.
Parent: Are you sure it was Annie?

Or:

Teacher: Misha has a hard time sitting still. She seems to have trouble focusing or staying on task.
Parent: Uh huh. So when did you say the field trip was?

Or:

Teacher: Patrick has a problem with telling the truth.
Parent: I've never seen that at home.

While you may understand a child better after meeting his or her parents, that fact alone will not ensure a good working relationship between parent and teacher.

Or:

> **Principal:** I'm suspending Logan for fighting.
>
> **Parent:** (*slamming her hand on table*) Listen! I've told all my kids—if someone hits you, you hit 'em back!

Or:

> **Parent:** My son got a ticket for parking in front of the gym!
>
> **Coach:** He parked in a handicapped space.
>
> **Parent:** He was late for practice.
>
> **Coach:** He's not handicapped.
>
> **Parent:** I think the laws discriminate against able-bodied persons. Just because he doesn't have a handicap, he's excluded from certain parking places. It's not fair!

Or:

> **Teacher:** I don't mind Todd bringing his iPad to class—in fact, it's great for taking notes. But he seems to spend time playing video games instead of paying attention.
>
> **Parent:** I'll ask him to turn the sound off.

Although you may understand a child better after meeting his or her parents, that fact alone will not ensure a good working relationship between parent and teacher. It may help you to gauge the extent of the challenge, however!

> *Just as good teachers must develop skills to work with all kinds of students, they must also develop skills to work with all kinds of parents.*

Like their offspring, all parents are different. Just as good teachers must develop skills to work with all kinds of students, they must also develop skills to work with all kinds of parents.

Even though individual parents are different, anyone who has worked with students and their parents for a few years can't help but notice that certain attitudes and points of view appear again and again. The names and faces change, but their expectations remain the same.

In the following chapters, we're going to look at some recurring types of parental behaviors that can make your life as a teacher miserable unless you are prepared to respond to them with confidence. If you have thought about how to handle unreasonable demands—what to say and how to say it—encounters with demanding parents can be less unnerving. Preparation will increase your chances of success.

You might take the advice of a golf coach to his players: "Think about your play and walk like you mean it."

Chapter 4
Pinocchio's Mom

Despite abundant evidence to the contrary, Pinocchio's Mom insists that her child doesn't lie. It is hard to tell whether she actually believes this or is foolish enough to think that others will actually believe it. She makes a teacher want to jump up and scream, "Liar, liar, pants on fire!"

There are more professional ways of handling this, however.

Pinocchio (or Pinocchia) is usually well aware that his mother will believe whatever he says. He is also often smart enough to take advantage of her readiness to defend him. If he gets in trouble in school, he understands that his best course of action is to get to his mother before the teacher does and spin his version of what happened.

Mom: (*on phone*) Pinocchio came home today and said that a boy in his class tripped him on the playground. He says you saw it and didn't do anything about it. He has a red mark on his forehead.

Teacher: That's not exactly what happened.

Mom: Pinocchio said the boy hit him, too. And you didn't do anything about it.

Teacher: As I said, that's not exactly what happened.

Mom: Are you calling my son a liar?

Teacher: I'm not calling anyone a liar. But what happened was that Pinocchio pushed Anthony off the swing.

Mom: That's not what Pinocchio said. And I know my son doesn't lie.

> *Pinocchio's Mom would much rather focus on what the teacher did or didn't do than on what her child did or didn't do.*

We all know where this is going—around and around and around. Pinocchio's Mom would much rather focus on what the teacher did or didn't do than on what her child did or didn't do. The teacher needs to help the parent refocus on the child's behavior.

Mom: Pinocchio came home today and said that a boy in his class tripped him on the playground. He says you saw it and didn't do anything about it. He has a red mark on his forehead.

Teacher: Well, we all know what a little liar your son is.

Ha ha! Just a little joke there. The teacher may *want* to say that, but of course she wouldn't unless she plans on leaving at the end of the year. Or sooner.

Here's another possibility:

Mom: Pinocchio came home today and said that a boy in his class tripped him on the playground. He says you saw it and didn't do anything about it. He has a red mark on his forehead.

Teacher: Yup, that's me. I let them do whatever they want.

Gotcha again! Remember that the first rule when dealing with irate parents is, "No sarcasm!" (It should also be parents' first rule in dealing with teachers, of course.) Got that? No sarcasm!

Here's a more productive way of handling the conversation:

Mom: Pinocchio came home today and said that a boy in his class tripped him on the playground. He says you saw it and didn't do anything about it. He has a red mark on his forehead.

Teacher: Did he give you any more specifics?

Mom: No, just that the boy tripped him.

Teacher: Did he say which boy?

Mom: (*shouting to Pinocchio*) Pin! She wants to know which kid tripped you . . . (*to the teacher*) . . . Anthony. He says a kid named Anthony tripped him.

Teacher: And when was this?

Mom: After lunch. Today.

Teacher: And he says I saw it?

Mom: Yes. And you didn't do anything.

Teacher: Did he tell you where on the playground this happened?

Mom: (*to Pinocchio*) She wants to know where it happened. (*to the teacher*) He doesn't remember.

Teacher: Well, we had a small incident on the playground today when Pinocchio pushed Anthony off the swing. I did see that.

Mom: (*a little doubtful*) That's not the way he tells it.

Teacher: Well, you may want to ask him about that. And I'll be happy to talk to him about it tomorrow.

Focus on specifics: who, what, when, where, and how. Even the most gullible parent does not want to be made to look like a fool. Refuse to be sucked into a debate about who is telling the truth. It isn't about who's lying, the teacher or the student, but about what actually happened.

Let's try another example:

Mom: Pinocchia says you gave her a zero for her research paper.

Teacher: She didn't hand anything in.

Mom: Pinocchia says she left it on your desk when you were out of the room.

Teacher: I didn't find a paper on my desk.

Mom: Are you saying my daughter is lying?

Okay, what's the teacher's next response?

a. Yup, like a rug.
b. Lying? Just look at her nose!
c. When exactly did she say she left it on my desk?

> *Refuse to be sucked into a debate about who is telling the truth.*

25

You're right. *Think* the first two, but *say* the third. Also keep in the back of your mind that, despite evidence to the contrary, you could be wrong. Try to keep an open mind and follow up with questions like these:

- What was the title of her paper?
- Did it have a cover?
- Why didn't she hand it in when I collected the rest of the papers?
- Why didn't she tell me she left it on the desk?

If this is the first time Pinocchia has tried this trick, or if there is even the slightest possibility in your own mind that she could be telling the truth, you will probably end up accepting a late paper. Raise enough questions, though, so that there is significant doubt in the parent's mind that Pinocchia actually did what she claimed she did. You also need to make it clear that this is a one-time ploy for Pinocchia. Use the magnanimous approach:

Teacher: I suppose it's possible that a paper could have been left in the room, but I just don't know how that could have happened. However, what I will do is allow Pinocchia until Friday to turn in another copy.

Some teachers may think that this response is caving in and "letting the kid get away with it." Well, maybe. But it's important to keep your eye on the prize: Pinocchia still has to do the assignment. She also knows not to try this trick with you again.

In my experience, there is a greater likelihood of a positive outcome in conversations with Pinocchia's mom if the student is present. If she is, I recommend that you talk directly to the student. I have a theory that it's easier for a student to lie to her mother than to you.

Pinocchia's Mom: My daughter said you wouldn't help her after school.
Teacher: *(directly to student)* I said I wouldn't help you?
Pinocchia: You said you didn't have time.
Teacher: *(to the student)* When was that?
Pinocchia: Last Tuesday.
Teacher: Oh, I remember. I told you we had a faculty meeting.
Pinocchia: *(silence)*
Teacher: Do you remember I said I'd help you the next day?
Pinocchia: No.
Teacher: You don't remember that I said to come by on Wednesday?

Pinocchia: (*silence*)

Teacher: (*to the parent*) I always offer extra help sessions on Wednesdays.

Mom: Pinocchia, is that right? Were you supposed to go on Wednesday?

Pinocchia: Maybe . . .

On occasion, Pinocchia will have already gotten herself in so deep with her mother that there is no way she can retreat. Kids often start out with a small lie and then for one reason or another—most likely just poor judgment—dig themselves a hole and can't find a way out.

Mom: Pinocchia said she didn't know she was failing.

Teacher: (*to Pinocchia*) You and I talked about this last week.

Pinocchia: You didn't say I was *failing*.

Teacher: I told you that you had a 52 average.

Pinocchia: But you didn't say I was *failing*.

Mom: I just think that you weren't very clear to Pinocchia.

At this point the teacher will want to say, " What do you think 52 means? That you're on the honor roll?" Instead, she will understand that Pinocchia is in over her, ah, nose.

Teacher: Well, then let's be clear now. You're failing math because you don't do your homework. You're a smart girl, but you don't do the work.

Mom: Pinocchia, is that right? You're not doing the work?

Pinocchia: Well, I do some of it.

Teacher: Some of it isn't good enough. You need to do all of it. Now, how about coming in after school on Wednesday?

Mom: She'll be there.

With younger children, it still helps if the child is present, but you have to be careful not to look like a bully:

Mom: Pinocchio says you said he cheated on the spelling test. Pinocchio would never cheat.

Teacher: Pinocchio, tell your mother what happened on the test.

Pinocchio: I already told her.

Mom: He said he was just asking for a tissue.

Teacher: Is that right? Is that what happened?

Mom: He has allergies.

Teacher: There are tissues on my desk. Pinocchio, you know that, right?

Pinocchio: (*He nods.*)

Teacher: So you don't have to ask anyone for anything during a test, right?

Pinocchio: (*He nods.*)

Teacher: So how about if you study, and we take the test again tomorrow?

Mom: It doesn't seem fair, but okay.

Watch for signs that the parent or student is allowing your point.

This technique is something I call, "delivering the message." Sometimes teachers make the mistake of believing that they have to get a complete confession out of a student. They seem to think it's not over until Pinocchio screams, "Okay! Okay! You got me, copper! I lied! I cheated!" Then he's cuffed and led away.

There's no need for all of this drama nor for students to be completely humiliated when they make the kinds of mistakes all youngsters make. (Of course, I'm talking here of errors in youthful judgment, not the serious kinds of mistakes that end up with kids being suspended from school or worse.) When you focus on delivering the message, all you need is acknowledgment that the message has been received. For example, in the previous conversation Pinocchio tacitly admitted his error with a nod, and the teacher let it go. She avoided putting the child in a place where he had no choice but to continue to lie to save face.

Here's another example:

Mom: Pinocchia said she didn't know the project was due Friday.

Teacher: Pinocchia, were you here on Monday?

Pinocchia: Yeah.

Teacher: That's the day I went over the assignment.

Pinocchia: I don't remember.

Mom: Five days doesn't seem like a very long time for the assignment.

Teacher: Well, I have to tell you that most students got it done.

Pinocchia: I didn't hear you.
Teacher: So what do you need to get the project finished?

Watch for signs that the parent or student is allowing your point. When Pinocchia says, "I didn't hear you," in the previous example, the teacher moves on to resolution. Pinocchia doesn't dispute what the teacher says, and, in actuality, subtly accepts some of the blame. The teacher doesn't have to add, "As usual, you weren't paying attention," or, "Everyone else seemed to hear it," or, "Maybe you were talking instead of listening," or any of the other things that teachers have been saying to kids for 100 years or so, with the same dull effect. None of those observations will help and will only push Pinocchia and her mother further away.

The teacher simply makes sure her message is delivered and understood: "The assignment was clear and you, Pinocchia, didn't do it." There is a much greater chance of amicable resolution to a problem if the teacher can recognize when the message has been received and leave it at that. Remember, you should be looking for changes in behavior, not punitive damages.

Of course, there are serious situations that do require the student to admit to wrongdoing—fighting, bullying, harassment, and so on. Delivering the message is a technique for garden-variety misunderstandings. However, any time a student's lie impugns your professionalism, ethics, intelligence, or morals, you have the obligation and the right to defend yourself.

One other thing: You only deliver the message once. If a student does the same thing a second time, all bets are off.

Mom: (*a month later*) Pinocchia didn't know that the test was Friday.
Teacher: Pinocchia, how did it happen that you didn't know?
Pinocchia: I don't know. I just didn't.
Teacher: I announced it in class and it was written on the board.
Pinocchia: I didn't see it.
Mom: Is there some way she can retake the test?
Teacher: I'm sorry. She will have other opportunities to improve her grade. As you know, we've dealt with this issue before. Pinocchia needs to write down her assignments. Maybe you could check at home to see if she does that.

> *Sometimes teachers make the mistake of believing that they have to get a complete confession out of a student.*

Here are a few points to keep in mind when dealing with Pinocchio's Mom:

- Keep focused on specifics: who, what, when, where, how. Don't allow charges to go unquestioned.
- Have your own data clear and handy. If it's a problem of assignments not being completed, know what was assigned and when. If it's a question of a grade, have ready the rubric you used or a copy of the test. Although there are times when a teacher can be completely caught off guard by a parental complaint, most teachers have a pretty good idea of what an issue is going to be when a concerned parent calls.
- If the student is present, talk to him or her directly in front of the parent. The older the student, the more direct you can be. With young children, it doesn't take much for the teacher to look like a bully. With older students, you can exert a little more pressure, but you'll want to be sure that your goal is fact-finding, not defending yourself.
- Refuse to be sucked in to a confrontation over the child's truthfulness. If the parent asks an inflammatory question like, "Are you calling my child a liar?" ignore the challenge. Instead, focus your response on the issue: "We're trying to find out what exactly happened here."
- Remember that you can "deliver the message" without getting a full confession and still get the results you want.

Pinocchio's mom will rarely admit that her child, like most, sometimes lies. She doesn't know that for kids it's a survival skill, not necessarily a character flaw at this point. Nearly all of them will grow out of it.

Those who don't will have bright political futures.

Refuse to be sucked in to a confrontation over the child's truthfulness.

Chapter 5
Caped Crusader

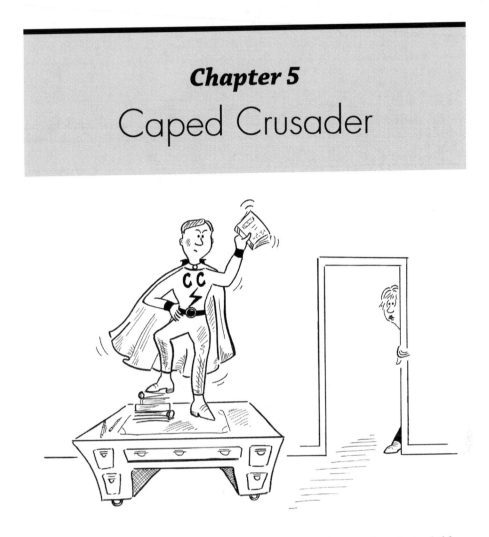

All parents have the right and responsibility to know what their children are learning. The Caped Crusader, however, believes his ideas or principles should be embraced by everyone. He is more than willing to fight for his ideas so that they can be applied throughout the school district.

A frequent target for the Crusader is the school curriculum. It is important to recognize that the Crusader may honestly disagree with a book choice a teacher makes and may legitimately protest having his child read it. In fact, he may have the right to *insist* that his child not read a particular book. What he doesn't have, however, is the right to choose for all of the other students in the class.

A typical conversation with the Crusader goes something like this:

Crusader: We have a problem with the book you're making the class read.

Teacher: Really? What kind of problem?

Crusader: We think it's not appropriate for children to read.

Teacher: Why is that?

Crusader: Well, the language, for one thing. And what happens in the book.

Teacher: Have you read the book?

Crusader: I didn't have to. I know what it says. And I know I speak for a lot of parents who aren't happy about your choice but just don't have the courage to say anything.

Teacher: No one's ever complained before.

Crusader: Like I said, people are afraid. I'm concerned not just for my child, but for everyone's child. Nobody should be subjected to a book like this.

For some beleaguered teachers, the thought that they might be striking fear in the heart of anyone, especially parents, seems a stretch. They might be tempted to ask, "Just what, exactly, are these people afraid of?" The response, however, would probably be, "They are afraid to say."

A teacher might be inclined to ignore the Crusader as just another wing-nut complaining about a book he hasn't even read. That would be a mistake. Annoying as it might be, he may be a test case for other parents who are not happy with a particular book choice and who may, in fact, become a critical mass if the issue isn't resolved to satisfaction.

The Crusader often likes to imply that he speaks for many, many others, so it's important to clarify whom he actually represents, right from the beginning.

Crusader: We have a problem with the book you're making the class read.

Teacher: I'm not sure who "we" is. Can you clarify?

Crusader: Well, I have a problem. And my wife.

Teacher: Oh, I see. You and your wife are unhappy with our book choice. What is your concern?

Crusader: Well, the language, for one thing.

Teacher: It's true that there are words in this book that we ordinarily wouldn't use in the classroom.

Crusader: So why are you making the students read them?

The Crusader often likes to imply that he speaks for many, many others, so it's important to clarify whom he actually represents, right from the beginning.

Teacher: It is my feeling that the topic of the book—a young man who manages to overcome great obstacles—could be helpful to many students.

Crusader: Well, I don't want Jane reading this stuff.

Teacher: No problem. I can find an alternate book for her.

> *It is important to limit the conversation to the parents at hand.*

It is important to limit the conversation to the parents at hand. Here's another way this conversation might go:

Crusader: We have a problem with the book you're making the class read.

Teacher: I'm not sure who "we" is.

Crusader: Well, I have a problem and so does my wife. And so do most of the members of my church.

Teacher: Well, let's start with the concerns that you and your wife have.

If a teacher plans to have students read a book that might be seen by some as controversial, it is a good idea to send a letter home to parents before students begin reading the book. The letter might say something like this:

Dear Parents:

Next semester we are going to read Chris Crutcher's *Whale Talk*. This book contains some mature language, but it is part of our study of personal courage. It is the story of how a group of high school students who see themselves as social misfits manage to accomplish a goal that changes their lives.

If you would prefer your child not read this book, please let me know and I will assign him or her an alternate choice.

Sincerely,
Teacher

By pointing out the mature language ahead of time, a teacher gives parents an opportunity to opt out without confrontation. Sometimes that will head off any problem. Other times it will not.

Parents do have a right to review what their child reads and to question a teacher's choices. They do have the right to speak for themselves and their child. They do not have the right to speak for everyone else and their children. To deal with parents who want to control everyone, most school districts have a policy on censorship in place. All teachers and librarians should know exactly what that policy says in case they have to remind their principal. Most policies spell out the process by which a book can be challenged. Many begin with a questionnaire that requires that the parent identify his or her specific objections to the book—something that cannot be accomplished if he hasn't read it.

If your school does not have a policy on censorship, I strongly recommend that you talk to your principal or librarian about developing one. Some schools put together a task force composed of teachers, library media specialists, administrators, and parents to examine policies on censorship and make recommendations to the school board. Sample policies can be obtained from organizations such as the American Association of School Librarians and the National Council of Teachers of English. You can also ask other local school districts for copies of their policies.

Parents do have a right to review what their child reads and to question a teacher's choices.

But what if your school doesn't have a policy in place and your principal doesn't want one? What if he or she prefers—in a worst-case scenario—to be the lone arbitrator on a book-by-book basis? If that is the case, you will want to make sure that you keep your principal apprised of your reading list and your CD/video list well in advance of classroom use. Although doing so risks preemptive censorship, you absolutely do not want to go it alone without administrative support if a parent seriously objects to one of your choices. These kinds of conflicts can quickly escalate, and you do not want to have to appear at a board of education meeting trying to explain your curriculum choices in front of a hostile crowd. If you find yourself in an intolerable situation that seriously compromises your academic freedom, it's better to look for another job than to try to defend yourself without district support.

Sometimes—because of a community's values or the lack of courage on the part of an administrator—a censorship policy is ignored, and a book is removed from the library shelves or from a teacher's reading list. If it happens to you, you may be forced to choose another book—or choose another school district. If you choose another book, remember to tell your students the reason that the book you chose was banned—not, "A group of pinheads who can barely read said we can't read this," but "The district has decided that we will remove this book, based on parental objections." If students want details, you can say, "I recommend that you talk to your parents." Stop there. You do not want to risk being quoted out of context and thereby inflaming emotions.

Over the years, various communities have banned all kinds of books, many of which have been recognized as classics—*The Adventures of Tom Sawyer, To Kill a Mockingbird, Flowers for Algernon, Anne Frank: The Diary of a Young Girl, Tales of a Fourth Grade Nothing*—the list, unfortunately, goes on and on. We typically don't think of librarians as being a subversive group, but several I know routinely schedule "Banned Book Week," during which these and other such books are placed on prominent display in the school library. "Celebrate the First Amendment," the sign says. "Read a banned book!" Most kids love it. Some parents don't.

We have all known or read about teachers who have found themselves the target of various groups associated with the religious right. (Maybe there's also a "religious left," but I've never seen them picketing a school to have students read more books promoting tolerance, diversity, and inclusiveness or carrying signs proclaiming "Darwin Was Right!" Maybe they need to get organized . . .). This is a conservative time in education, and the current focus is on assessment and accountability. For some religious and political groups, the focus is also on conforming to standards that they set for themselves and would like to set for everybody else. In addition, teachers in general in some states have been political targets, seeing their benefits abridged, their salaries capped, and their numbers reduced. So it's important to think and plan carefully and not put yourself at risk unnecessarily. To be clear: I'm not suggesting that you back away from your chosen curriculum choices. I am saying that you prepare the groundwork first if you suspect there could be a problem.

The pendulum will eventually swing back, of course. I'm hopeful that it won't be long before we are able to take a more reasoned, moderate approach to education—an approach that will include a certain amount of academic flexibility and a recognition that not everything a child learns has be tested—nor can it be. In the meantime, teachers need to be proactive in alerting parents and administrators to possible controversy so that they do not end up having to defend their classroom choices and their jobs without the support of their school system.

Besides trying to influence the curriculum to conform to his personal beliefs, the Caped Crusader may also want to influence other classroom practices for his own benefit or for the benefit of his own child.

Crusader: Ben has a hard time getting up in the morning.

Teacher: He's missing essential reading instruction several times a week.

Crusader: I don't see why you can't just wait to start reading instruction until Ben gets here.

> *Teachers need to be proactive in alerting parents and administrators to possible controversy.*

Clearly, no teacher should have to readjust the instruction schedule for everyone because one child wants to sleep in. And when you tell the Crusader that some people might see Ben's chronic tardiness as parental neglect, you will be on firm ground. The Crusader may not like it, but it's your professional obligation.

I do need to point out that on occasion, the Crusader will actually have a valid concern, one that may require understanding and creativity on the part of the teacher:

Crusader: I understand that you're taking all of the fifth graders to the petting zoo.

Teacher: Yes, we've just finished our animal unit, and we're looking forward to seeing the animals we've read about.

Crusader: You know, my son Donnie is allergic to animal hair.

Teacher: He is?

Crusader: Yes. So he won't be able to go. I don't think it's fair that he isn't able to participate in a class activity. He's going to feel left out. I would think that if one child can't go, none of them should.

This kind of issue requires a sensitive response. "Okay, then, we'll call it off" isn't an option if you have 25 other 10-year-olds waiting to pet Bambi. Calling it off will not improve Donnie's popularity with his classmates, either. Instead, you might try this approach:

Teacher: Would you like to come along with us that day? Maybe there are some things your son can do on the trip. There are interesting displays inside the farmhouse and there's a video, too. The decision would be yours.

It's not always easy for the teacher to balance the needs of the minority against the rights of the majority, but it's the right thing to do. The thoughtful teacher will strive to find a way for all kids to participate in some meaningful way, if at all possible.

Sometimes, however, despite our best efforts, a parent cannot be assuaged. Suppose the conversation goes more like this:

Teacher: Maybe you'd like to come along that day. Maybe there are some things your son could do, and you would know what those things are.

Crusader: Look, I can't take off work for something like this. There's no way my child can go, and I insist you cancel the trip.

Teacher: I'm sorry. That's just not possible.

Crusader: Well, I'll just have to see the principal.

Teacher: You need to do what you think is right.

If you're lucky, the principal will support your choice. If not, the principal can explain the situation to the parents of the other students so that your choices can be seen as school policy and not as your individual choice.

As a side note, however, I'd like to add that today's teacher should be familiar with students' medical issues as they affect classroom activities, so as to avoid some of these conflicts. If you know ahead of time that certain children have asthma, allergies, or any condition that could affect their participation in a school

> *It's not always easy for the teacher to balance the needs of the minority against the rights of the majority, but it's the right thing to do.*

activity, you can take their needs into account when planning. When you plan ahead, parents will be grateful that you considered the needs of their child, rather than angry that their child may be excluded.

Sometimes teachers, especially new ones, are reluctant to bring problems with insistent parents to their principal because they are afraid that it will make them look incompetent. This is a mistake, unless the principal herself is incompetent. (If so, you've got even bigger problems.) Part of a principal's job is to deal with irate parents, so let her do it. Another part of the principal's job is running interference so that you can do your job. If the Crusader continues to be a problem, refer him to the principal on a regular basis.

If you really can't go to the principal, a veteran colleague may be able to help. He or she has probably weathered similar situations and not only can advise you but also can be physically present at conferences—as both a buffer and a witness in a possibly volatile situation.

Here are some points to remember when dealing with the Crusader:

- All parents have the right to review what their child is learning and to opt out of some activities. Don't take their objections personally.
- Avoid some confrontations by being proactive and alerting parents to classroom assignments that might be viewed as controversial. Parents appreciate knowing about things before they happen. Although they may not agree with your choices, they won't think that you're trying to push something past them without their noticing. By the same token, if parents ignore the information and protest your choice afterward, you can always point to the fact that they were alerted beforehand.
- Schools need to have a policy on censorship. If your school doesn't have one, see if you can promote developing one. It's for your own protection.
- If problems persist, refer the Crusader to your principal.

It's important to remember that the Crusader sometimes has a point, even if his solution is unacceptable. Keep an open mind, and you may be able to work out a reasonable compromise. If you can't, you need to decide what is important to you and what is best for the kids. It's not your job to resolve every difference with

Just as good teachers must develop skills to work with all kinds of students, they must also develop skills to work with all kinds of parents.

a parent; it's your job to teach. Get your principal involved and let him or her work it out.

If you can win over the Caped Crusader, you can harness his energy to do good and vanquish evil. When he believes in a cause, he can be a tireless worker. If you're lucky, you can get him to channel his efforts toward raising money for new playground equipment . . . or maybe even garnering support for the school budget.

Chapter 6

Ms. "Quit Picking on My Kid"

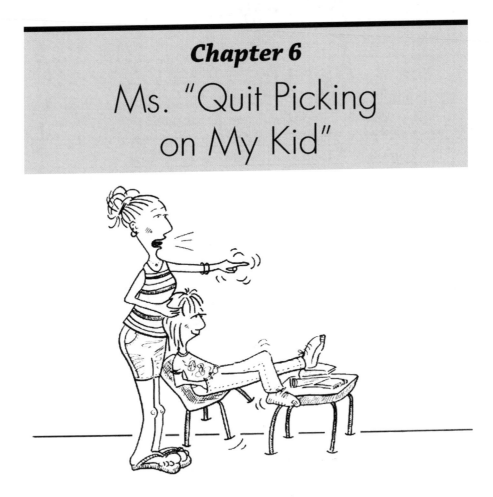

Whenever a conflict arises, whatever the circumstances, some parents will accuse the teacher of picking on their child. Even when the parent admits that her child's behavior was unacceptable, she will argue that everyone else's was, too. "Unless you're going to punish everyone," she will tell the teacher, "you shouldn't be singling out my child."

If you do punish the whole class, she will ask you to single her child out as the only one who doesn't deserve it. (Of course, punishing the whole class is a bad idea anyway, and I'd like to think that there are no teachers left on the planet who would ever do that.)

Here's an example of a conversation with Ms. "Quit Picking on My Kid!":

Ms. Quit: I understand you told Amanda that her T-shirt wasn't acceptable and she couldn't wear it to school again.

Teacher: Yes, that's true.

Ms. Quit: Well, what about all the other kids who wear the same kind of shirts?

Teacher: What other kids?

Ms. Quit: I could stand in the hall and see 10 kids with shirts worse than hers. Why are you just picking on my daughter?

Teacher: You can find 10 kids whose T-shirts say something worse than "I put the F-U in Fun"?

Ms. Quit: It's part of a song.

Teacher: We don't let kids wear T-shirts like that.

Ms. Quit: I think she has a right to wear whatever she wants. If everyone else can, so can she.

Of course, the first question in the teacher's mind is usually, "Why would a parent defend her child's 'right' to be offensive?" The second question is, "What in the world are the lyrics to the *rest* of that song?"

I can't answer either one of those questions, but I do know that the teacher in the example above allowed herself to be distracted from the main issue. The school rules about dress are not personal, and they apply to all kids. Let's try it again:

Ms. Quit: I understand you told Amanda her T-shirt was not acceptable and she couldn't wear it to school again.

Teacher: Yes, that's true. Our school dress code says that students may not wear T-shirts with messages or pictures that are suggestive or offensive.

Ms. Quit: Well, what about the other kids?

Teacher: The issue here is Amanda's shirt. It violates the dress code about offensive messages.

Ms. Quit: Other kids do the same thing.

Teacher: The dress code prohibits shirts like these.

Ms. Quit: I think you're singling Amanda out.

Teacher: The dress code applies to everyone. No offensive T-shirts.

Ms. Quit: I could go outside and pick out 10 kids with the same kind of shirt.

Teacher: Let me give you a copy of the dress code.

The " broken record" technique—repeating the same thing in different ways and staying on message—isn't new, but is still effective. It requires self-discipline. The teacher

> *The "broken record" technique—repeating the same thing in different ways and staying on message—isn't new, but is still effective.*

must refuse to be drawn into battle over whether or not the student has been singled out.

Here's another example:

Teacher: We can't tolerate Brian's use of the F word in class.

Parent: He's not the only one who swears. I hear it in the halls all the time.

Teacher: His language isn't appropriate for class time.

Parent: Other kids swear.

Teacher: He will not be allowed to use language like that in my classroom.

Parent: What about all the other kids?

Teacher: I don't want any kids swearing in my classroom and that includes Brian.

I have to admit that some parents have a point when they wonder whether a school rule is being applied equally to all students. What they don't understand is that it is tough, if not impossible, to catch every dress code violation or to correct every student who uses foul language. Also, like it or not, some kids develop a track record that makes them more likely than others to be cited for yet another violation.

That being said, teachers need to be vigilant about applying the rules as equitably as possible. However, let's face it: Even the most "objective" rules are open to interpretation. Here's another version of the conversation between Amanda's mother and the teacher:

Ms. Quit: I understand you told Amanda her T-shirt was not acceptable and she couldn't wear it to school again.

Teacher: Yes, that's true. Our school dress code says that students may not wear T-shirts with messages or pictures that are suggestive or offensive.

Ms. Quit: Well, what about the other kids?

Teacher: The issue here is Amanda's shirt. It violates the dress code about offensive messages.

Ms. Quit: Other kids do the same thing. Nobody says anything to them.

Teacher: You know, it's not always possible to catch every violation every day. We do our best to make sure that kids dress appropriately, but I'm not going to tell you that we see everything. We have 800 students in this building, and it's hard to catch everything. But we try.

Ms. Quit: I just don't want you to be picking on only Amanda.

Teacher: I understand. But I'd appreciate it if Amanda didn't wear that shirt again.

Ms. Quit: Okay. But you need to look at the other kids, too.

> *It's not a bad idea for a teacher to admit that, despite her best efforts, the results are not always perfect.*

It's not a bad idea for a teacher to admit that, despite her best efforts, the results are not always perfect. It's even likely that Amanda herself has slipped by unnoticed in the past—maybe with this same shirt. However, part of the teacher's job is enforcing the dress code, and she needs to do it. It's not easy, and I can tell you as a former high school administrator that when a student is sent to the office during eighth period for inappropriate attire, the kid had already gone through the entire day without anyone saying anything. It's a tough argument to make to the parents when only one out of 8 teachers has either noticed the shirt or decided to do something—so we might as well admit we're not perfect.

Sometimes the issue isn't dress, but behavior. Some parents may believe that their children are being denied a "right" they think others have:

Parent: I'd like to know what the problem is with Ralph waiting for his friends after school.

Principal: If students don't have a reason to be here, they need to go home when classes are over. No loitering.

Parent: Ralph has a reason to be here. He's waiting for his friends.

Principal: That's not a reason.

Parent: What do you mean, "That's not a reason"? Waiting for his friends isn't a reason?

Principal: Students staying after school need to be with a teacher or a coach. They just can't hang around in the halls.

Parent: Like he's the only one in the halls after school! Come on!

It's important to remember that parents don't have the advantage of seeing how their child's behavior multiplied by 20 or 50 or 100 other kids plays out. One kid waiting for a friend after school truly is no big deal. Fifty kids is. Let's try it again:

Parent: Ralph has a reason to be here. He's waiting for his friends.

Principal: We can't allow students to be in the school unsupervised. It's for our protection and for theirs.

Parent: I don't see how waiting for his friends is a problem.

Principal: It wouldn't be a problem if it were just Ralph. But we have a number of kids who want to hang around after school unsupervised and that *is* a problem. It's an opportunity for kids to get into trouble, and I don't want that to happen to Ralph.

Parent: Well, I'm not sure I agree, but I see what you're saying.

Most parents rarely think about what would happen if everyone did what they want to do or what their child wants to do. This is understandable; they are focusing on their own needs. As teachers, though, we know that behavior can be contagious. If we let one second grader get a drink of water during the spelling test, the next thing you know we have a drought. If one kid throws up on the school bus, we're one block away from a barf-o-rama.

> *We need to help parents understand that rules are made for everyone's benefit, even though it may not look like it at first glance.*

We need to help parents understand that rules are made for everyone's benefit, even though it may not look like it at first glance. An example:

Mom: I'll come down to the classroom to pick up Curt for his allergy shots.

Teacher: Actually, our school policy is that you should go to the nurse's office, and she will call Curt down.

Mom: I'd rather just come down to the room. It's quicker.

Teacher: We try not to have parents come to the room. It's a disruption for the other students.

Mom: I don't see how picking up my own child is such a big deal. Going to the nurse's office is an inconvenience.

Teacher: I understand. But we have lots of students who have doctor or dentist appointments during the day. If all parents came directly to their child's room, we'd have a steady stream of interruptions. Also, for safety reasons in this day and age, we really don't want a lot of adults wandering the halls.

Mom: Oh. I guess I hadn't thought about that.

If you take the time to explain to a parent why a particular rule must be followed, most will accept the idea, even if they don't agree with it. Unfortunately, this is not always the case:

Parent: You had no right to take Alicia's cell phone away.

Teacher: She was talking on the phone during my math class.

Parent: She was talking to me! She just called to tell me she'd be late from school.

Teacher: I understand. But we were in the middle of math class. We can't have kids interrupting class with phone calls.

Parent: Other students have phones in class. You are singling her out!

Teacher: Other students do have phones. But she was the only one talking on one.

Parent: That phone is her personal property, and I want it back right now!

Teacher: Of course. Here it is. As I told her, she can have it back after school. Please remind her not to use it in class.

Parent: I'm not reminding her of anything.

Despite the parent's parting comment, it's unlikely that Alicia will use her phone again in math class unless she decides to deliberately challenge her teacher's authority. If that happens, the stakes are raised, and the problem needs to be moved to the principal's office.

Up to this point we've talked about dealing with parents who think their child is being singled out because of the child's behavior. Sometimes, however, if a student is not performing as well as the parents would like academically, the parents may accuse the teacher of singling the student out in other ways. Parents may complain that the teacher is expecting more (or less) from their child than from other students or that the teacher is being harder (or easier) on him than other students. The bottom line is that parents may believe that

If you take the time to explain to a parent why a particular rule must be followed, most will accept the idea, even if they don't agree with it.

their child is not getting the breaks given to other students. Here's an example:

Teacher: I just don't think Sam will be successful in AP English next year. I think he should stay with regular English.

Parent: We want him to take AP.

Teacher: Does he want to take AP?

Parent: It doesn't matter what he wants.

Teacher: AP takes a lot of work and effort. Sam doesn't seem willing to work hard in English.

Parent: He'll work hard for teachers he likes. He feels that you pick on him.

Teacher: I don't pick on him. I do get after him about his homework.

Parent: He's not the only one who doesn't do it.

Parents need to be reassured that their child is not being singled out or excluded for no reason. They need to feel secure that the teacher's recommendations are in their child's best interests and not simply the result of the teacher's need to be right.

Here's a more productive way to handle the previous conversation:

Parent: Sam works hard for teachers he likes. He feels that you pick on him.

Teacher: I'm sorry he feels that way. I do get after him about his homework.

Parent: He's not the only one who doesn't do it.

Teacher: I know. I wish I only had one student I had to get after. But that's my job, and I'm sure you wouldn't like it if I just ignored it.

Parent: Well, what about AP?

Teacher: If you really want him to take the course, he can sign up. I'll meet with him individually and talk to him about the course expectations.

Parent: I'll talk to him, too.

I strongly suggest that if a parent insists on his child taking a course over the teacher's objection, the teacher should let him sign up. Maybe the teacher's wrong—he should hope that he is. Maybe taking the AP course isn't the best thing for the student, but it won't be the worst thing that ever happened to him, either.

It isn't always easy to deflect a parent's charge that a teacher is picking on her child. After all, what the parent is really questioning is the teacher's fairness, even professionalism. Many teachers naturally become defensive. However, defensiveness that results in responding directly to a parent's challenge is the worst response.

Parent: Penny says you pick on her when she's not paying attention.
Teacher: I don't pick on her.
Parent: Well, she feels picked on. She thinks you don't like her.
Teacher: I do like her.
Parent: She thinks you let other kids get away with things, but not her.
Teacher: I don't let other kids get away with things.
Parent: Well, that's how she feels—that you pick on her.
Teacher: I don't pick on her.

"Yes, you do! No, I don't!"—sounds like two kids on the playground. Clearly, simple denial doesn't work. Here's a different approach:

Parent: Penny says you pick on her in class.
Teacher: What does that mean?
Parent: I don't know. She just says you pick on her.
Teacher: Hmmm. I wonder how she defines being picked on.
Parent: I don't really know the specifics. She doesn't say.
Teacher: Well, that would be important. I'd like to know what she means.
Parent: I guess you'll have to ask her.
Teacher: Maybe you could ask her. Or maybe we could meet with her together. This is something I take seriously, because I work hard to treat kids fairly.
Parent: Well, maybe I'll talk to her and then let you know.

Rather than accepting the charge on the face of it, a good technique for a teacher to employ is to ask the parent to define her terms. What does "picking on" mean to your child? That you won't let her talk while you're talking? That you won't accept late homework? That you expect her to keep her hands and feet to herself? Rather than quickly trying to defend your actions, it's a

Parents need to be reassured that their child is not being singled out or excluded for no reason.

48

good idea to stop, think, and then ask questions first to clarify what exactly the parent means.

Don't deny. Clarify.

Parent: John says you give way too much homework. He just can't get it all done.

Teacher: I don't give too much homework.

No, no, no! Remember: Don't deny. Clarify.

Parent: John says you give way too much homework. He just can't get it all done.

Teacher: How much homework does he think he could do?

Parent: Ahhhhhhh . . . geez, I don't know. An hour?

Teacher: Well, I typically give about a half hour.

Parent: Well, he says it takes him an hour.

Teacher: Do you check his assignments in the evening?

Parent: Not usually. Should I?

Teacher: It might not be a bad idea. Maybe you could monitor his homework for a week or so, and then we can meet again.

If you can remember that both you and the parent want the same thing—the child's success in school—you may be able to stay out of the win-lose arena. It's not easy, but it can be done by refusing to be defensive. Don't respond directly to a parent's accusations.

It's also helpful to keep in the back of your mind that the parent just might have a point. You may think it's an itty-bitty point, but it's a point nonetheless. Ignoring that possibility can leave you blindsided and may exacerbate what begins as a small problem. So let's consider this possibility for a moment: What if the parent is right?

So far in this chapter we've talked about how to respond professionally when parents accuse a teacher of picking on their child or singling him out for one reason or another. We've talked about how parents can have myopic vision when it comes to their own child, finding it difficult to imagine how their child's behavior multiplied by 50 kids can present a problem in the school. We also talked about how school rules are generally made for the greater good, so that all children can learn without disruption or interruption. We believe that school rules should be based on the golden mean: What would the result be if everyone took this action?

Having said all of the above, I should point out that teachers still need to be careful about using that old chestnut, "If I let your child (fill in the blank), I'd have to let everyone's child (fill in the blank with the same words)." For example, "If I let your child bring a pony to school, I'd have to let everyone's child bring a pony." In this case, the parent can understand how (assuming that every child had a pony) it could be distracting with the noise and the manure and all. But in some cases, the parent may think, "Yeah, so what?" We need to be careful that the rules are really made for the good of the students, *not* for the convenience of the teacher.

A good technique for a teacher to employ is to ask the parent to define her terms.

The charge of singling kids out (or the converse, not responding to a child's individual needs) is among the most common complaints parents have. Before dismissing such a complaint as out of hand, it's a good idea to listen carefully and reflectively to be sure that your response isn't based on convenience or a need for control. Here's a worst-case example of what happens when a rule or procedure is not based on what's best for kids:

Parent: I'd like my daughter to be able to take whatever book she wants out of the library.

Librarian: I choose the books for second graders. She can pick from the second-grade shelf.

Parent: She can read at a 10th-grade level!

Librarian: If I let your daughter choose any book in the library, I'd have to let all of the second graders choose any book.

Parent: And the problem with that is . . . ?

Librarian: Not all second graders can read as well as your daughter. They would take out books they couldn't understand. And I'd be the one reshelving them.

Parent: What if I told you I don't care?

Librarian: Your daughter still has to pick from the second-grade books.

Behind each rule should be a genuine reason that isn't really based on our own comfort level but on the good of our classes as a whole. Basing decisions on what's best for the teacher instead of what's best for the students is simply wrong.

Here's another example of how a teacher's need to be in control can get in the way:

Parent: Zach occasionally has back spasms. He may need to get up and walk around.

Teacher: That could be a problem.

Parent: When he can move, he can listen. You may not think he's paying attention, but he is. He just needs to move.

Teacher: If I let Zach get up and move, I have to let all of the students do it.

Of course, that's not true. Kids know instinctively when another student has a special need of some kind. Most of them have an innate sense of fairness. If a child has a special need that we can easily accommodate, we should do it. Here's a more reasonable approach:

Parent: Zach occasionally has back spasms. He may need to get up and walk around.

Teacher: All he has to do is give me a little signal. We can make this work.

If we are unwilling to respond to a child's genuine need to be singled out for extra attention or assistance, then even supportive parents can be trained to become difficult.

Let's review the techniques to use with parents who accuse you of picking on their child or singling him or her out in a negative sense:

- Be a broken record. If it's a rule that you must enforce, stay on message. If it's behavior that simply cannot be tolerated—bullying, loitering, foul language, disrespect—teachers and administrators need to stay the course, but work to convince parents that the rules are applied the same way to all students.
- Help parents see that their child's behavior, multiplied by many students, can be a problem. One child arriving early can stand quietly in the doorway. Fifty kids need supervision.

It's also helpful to keep in the back of your mind that the parent just might have a point.

51

- Insist that parents define their terms. What does "picking on" look like? How long is an assignment that is "too long"?
- Make sure the rules are for the good of children and the school in general, not just for the teacher's convenience or need for control.
- Make adjustments for individual kids who need it, and don't worry about upsetting the classroom.

Parents sometimes act as if teachers and administrators like telling kids what they can or can't wear. Or that we like hounding kids to turn in their homework. Or that it's fun to have to defend your curriculum choices.

They're dead wrong, of course. Why would anyone spend all of those years in college just to spend a lifetime doing that?

Chapter 7
The Intimidator

Many people think that teachers can be intimidators—and they can be. The teacher who holds a student up to ridicule, bullies a student in gym class, yells at a first grader, or embarrasses or even threatens a student—none of these people belong in the classroom.

Parents can be intimidators in the classroom, too, although they are usually more subtle:

Teacher: Thanks for meeting with me, Mr. Kozinski.

Intimidator: Well, I hope you can make this quick, Alice.

Teacher: I'll do the best I can, but I really need to talk to you about Ronnie's behavior in class.

Intimidator: (*silence*)

Teacher: (*nervously*) He's very disrespectful.

Intimidator: (*silence*)

Teacher: He makes it difficult for the others to learn.

Intimidator: I really find that hard to believe.

Teacher: Yesterday, for example, he kept making monkey noises every time I turned my back.

Intimidator: You know, Alice, I have a lot more important things to do than hear about how my son makes monkey noises. It seems to me a good teacher wouldn't have that problem.

It is important to establish in a parent conversation that teacher and parent are equals. In the above conversation, the teacher calls the parent "Mr." while the parent calls the teacher "Alice." Instead of being a conversation between equals, it is more like a conversation between a patron in a restaurant and his server who wears a nametag. See how this changes the tone:

Teacher: Thanks for meeting with me, Mr. Kozinski.

Intimidator: Well, I hope you can make this quick, Alice.

Teacher: I know you're a busy person, Bob, so let me get right to it. Your son's grades are suffering because he is having trouble staying on task.

Intimidator: What does that mean?

Teacher: It means that instead of listening to directions, he's busy trying to entertain the other kids. I've talked to him several times, and I've moved him to the front of the room. I've even kept him after school. I think he needs to hear from you that he needs to settle down.

Intimidator: I'll tell him that.

Notice what the teacher does in this conversation:

- She immediately switches to a first-name basis. If the parent calls her Alice, she must be able to call him Bob.
- She acknowledges that Bob is busy and cuts to the chase.
- She focuses on the result of the child's behavior—low grades.
- She tells what actions she's already taken.
- She tells the parent specifically what she wants him to do.

Calling a parent by his or her first name may take a little courage, but with practice a teacher can do it. Before you meet with a parent or call him on the phone, it's a good idea to be sure you know his first name, just in case he decides

It is important to establish in a parent conversation that teacher and parent are equals.

to call you by yours. (A side note: It's never safe to assume that a parent's surname is the same as the child's, so always check.)

It's important that the teacher point out what she's done so far to correct the student's behavior. Talking to the parent shouldn't be the first step in dealing with an unruly child:

> *Talking to the parent shouldn't be the first step in dealing with an unruly child.*

Intimidator: How can you allow him to make monkey noises?

Teacher: I've spoken to him, and I've moved his seat to the front of the room. He's also lost playtime at the end of the day because of his behavior. I hate to send him home, but we're heading that way unless his behavior improves.

Intimidator: Ronnie and I will have a conversation, and you will see an improvement.

Intimidators may be used to getting what they want and are clear in their expectations for you. However, they may not be so clear when it comes to expectations for their child. Notice how the Intimidator in the following conversation puts all responsibility on the teacher and none on the child:

Intimidator: What does Beth have to do to raise her grade in this class?

Teacher: She'll need to get her homework in on time and study for the tests.

Intimidator: I would expect you to see that she does that.

Teacher: I will do my best, but some of it is up to her.

Intimidator: You're the teacher. It's your job to see that she works hard.

Intimidators are often people who are used to being in charge and telling subordinates what to do. Sometimes they view teachers not as professionals, but as public servants—with the emphasis on the servant part. Make sure you start out with and maintain a professional tone. It helps to remember that the Intimidator wouldn't dream of talking to his doctor the way he talks to his child's teacher. Imagine a conversation like this:

Intimidator: So I'll expect to see an improvement in my daughter's flu.

Doctor: Only if she takes her medicine and follows my instructions regarding rest.

Intimidator: I'm going out of town. I expect you to see that she does those things.

Doctor: Next patient!

Keep in mind that "medical model" when you meet with the Intimidator. Don't let the Intimidator get away with expecting you to do his job. It's useful to clearly point out the role that he has in helping his child be successful in school.

Intimidator: So I'll expect to see an improvement in Liz's grades.

Teacher: I will do my best to help her, but whether she improves depends on her. And you.

Intimidator: Me? You're the teacher!

Teacher: If you make it clear to Liz that you expect her best effort, then it will certainly help.

Intimidator: Well, I'm out of town a lot. I can talk to her, but it's still up to you to see that her work is done.

Teacher: I'll do my best. But no one is more effective with a child than her mother or father.

Intimidator: She knows what my expectations are.

Teacher: Good. It probably wouldn't hurt to remind her of them, though. And make sure she knows that we've talked and that you're aware of what she needs to do.

Intimidator: All right. But I'll be looking for some improvement in her grade the next time.

Teacher: I hope you tell her that.

Intimidator: You need to tell her that, too.

Teacher: Tell you what. Don't tell me how to do my job, and I won't tell you how to do yours.

Yes, you'll have to forgo the pleasure of that last line.

Intimidators will sometimes threaten teachers, saying that they will go to the principal or the superintendent or the school board if they don't get what they want. There's only one good response to such a threat:

Teacher: You need to do what you think is right.

Make sure you start out with and maintain a professional tone.

Never try to talk a parent out of going over your head. Intimidators can smell fear. "Do what you think is right" means, "I am sticking to my guns. If the principal wants me to do something different, I'll be answering to him and not to you." Then be sure to alert your supervisor that he or she may be getting a call.

Even when Intimidators raise the threat level with, "You'll hear from my lawyer," the response should be the same:

> *If a child commits a flagrant foul that results in discipline, call the parent before the student gets home.*

Teacher: You need to do what you think is right.

Sometimes the Intimidator will even make the Ultimate Threat:

Intimidator: Well, it looks like we'll just have to pull Evan out and send him to private school.
Teacher: Yippee! Woo hoo! Happy dance!

Of course, that's only going on in the teacher's head. In reality, here's what she should say:

Teacher: I'm sorry to hear that. I hope he'll like it.

Here are a few other ways for teachers to avoid or diffuse intimidating situations:

- The best defense is a good offense. If a child commits a flagrant foul that results in discipline, call the parent before the student gets home. If you wait, you may receive an angry call before you have a chance to tell the parent what really happened. Parents deserve the courtesy of a phone call, and it's better to put the errant student in the position of having to explain himself.
- Never force a child to call his parent to tell what he's done wrong while you stand right over him. This move is popular with some elementary and middle school teachers, but it can backfire. In the first place, it smacks of bullying on the part of the teacher. In the second place, the parent may balk at the implied expectation that she should respond in some predetermined way to what she is hearing from her child. Is she supposed to be angry? Apologetic? Disappointed? If she simply accepts the information to deal with when the child gets home, does

she look like she doesn't care? If you want to keep the lines of communication open and work with the parent to solve a problem, it is much better to deal with classroom issues as adults.

■ Try not to take an irate phone call at the end of the day. Parents sometimes overreact by calling the school as soon as the child gets off the bus and tells his story. If they believe their child has been wronged in some way, they may be too angry to engage in reasoned dialogue. Wait until the following morning when everyone has had time to cool off. Then you make the call. Don't wait for the parents to call a second time.

■ Do not give parents (or students) your home phone number or, God forbid, your cell phone number. Even if it seems like a good idea at the time, it is not. You need to separate your personal and professional lives. Besides, e-mail works just as well—maybe better—because you can open it or not, as you wish. (If you choose to respond by e-mail, NO SHOUTING!) Some teachers communicate with their students on Facebook, but check with your administrator before you do as some schools now prohibit it, worrying that it can make teachers and their students vulnerable to abuse. I suggest you give the idea some serious thought before moving forward.

Bullies are the same whether they're 6 or 46. It's sometimes hard to keep your wits about you when a bully challenges you. But remember: You have stood up to intimidating behavior before—perhaps your older brother, a college roommate, the head of your department, the sales clerk at the cosmetics counter, or the guy at the phone store who can't believe you haven't upgraded yet.

You're a teacher. You're brave by definition.

Chapter 8
The Stealth Zapper

Unlike the Intimidator, who lets you know exactly where he stands and what he wants, the Stealth Zapper gently implies that you (or maybe a colleague) aren't quite up to snuff. Her comments and criticisms fly so low under the radar that you may not realize you have been zapped until you stop to consider what she has said. She may appear innocent, but her words and actions can sting.

The Stealth Zapper can appear to be a big supporter of the school but only if it enhances her child's opportunities. She works hard to ingratiate herself with teachers if she thinks it might give her child an advantage. For example, if her child tries out for the musical, she will volunteer to be the accompanist for auditions. If her child gets a big part, look for this parent behind the scenes building sets, making costumes, and selling tickets at the door. If her child gets a smaller part, she will still be there, but she will probably be pointing out the director's mistakes at every opportunity. Conversations are likely to go something like this:

Stealth Zapper: It's too bad that Marion is so much taller than Harold Hill. It's kind of hard to believe they're a couple.

Teacher: (*thinking*) This is an eighth-grade production of *The Music Man*. All of the girls are taller than the boys! (*aloud*) Marion has the strongest voice in the class.

Stealth Zapper: I don't think you gave Brooklyn a chance to show you what she can really do.

Teacher: We listened to all of the students sing at auditions.

Stealth Zapper: Yes, but I think you were talking to someone during her audition.

Unlike the Intimidator, who puts an issue right on the table (or right in the teacher's face), the Stealth Zapper obliquely criticizes what the teacher has done and is more subtle in asking for what she wants. Here's another example of how she can catch a teacher off guard:

Stealth Zapper: Marjorie was so disappointed when you gave her a C– on her project.

Teacher: (*thinking*) What's the right answer to that? That's what she deserved? I'm sorry to disappoint her? She should have worked harder and gotten it in on time? And I didn't "give" her anything! (*aloud*) I'm sorry to hear that.

Stealth Zapper: She really didn't understand the directions. They weren't very clear.

Teacher: (*thinking*) We only went over them a million times! (*aloud*) I'm sorry to hear that.

Generally, the best approach with the Stealth Zapper is to deal with her directly, hold your ground, and be polite. Here's a better approach:

Stealth Zapper: Marjorie was really disappointed when you gave her a C– on her project.

Teacher: Really.

Stealth Zapper: She didn't understand the directions. They weren't very clear.

Teacher: I'm surprised to hear that. She never asked for clarification.

Stealth Zapper: You know how shy Marjorie is.

> *Generally, the best approach with the Stealth Zapper is to deal with her directly, hold your ground, and be polite.*

Teacher: Yes. But it's hard to know that a student doesn't understand something if she doesn't speak up.

Another ploy the Stealth Zapper uses to try to ingratiate herself with her child's current teacher is to subtly (or not so subtly) denigrate the last teacher her child had:

Stealth Zapper: Madison loves your class. Last year she had a really hard time in English.

Teacher: Really? Why is that?

Stealth Zapper: Mr. Johnson was so strict. He just had no sense of humor. Not like you, according to Madison.

The teacher may be trying to imagine either Madison or her mother appreciating a good sense of humor—or he may be wondering if either one would be amused to know that Mr. Johnson was his college roommate and best man at his wedding!

Comments about colleagues should also be dealt with directly, if possible. Here's an example:

Stealth Zapper: Miss Truman was so strict. None of the kids liked her. She just had no sense of humor. Madison thinks you're really funny.

Teacher: Well, I'm surprised. Miss Truman is known for her sense of humor. Kids usually love it.

But what if the last time Miss Truman laughed out loud was 1978, and her sense of humor is so dry that a good breeze would turn it to dust? You still need to avoid any appearance of agreeing with her criticism. If you aren't comfortable defending Miss Truman or another teacher, remember that an equally effective strategy is to just ignore the Stealth Zapper's personal observations and respond only to those that pertain to you.

Stealth Zapper: Miss Truman was so strict. She had no sense of humor. Not like you, according to Madison.

Teacher: I'm glad Madison gets my jokes. I enjoy having her in class.

No matter what you think of a colleague, you need to remain positive or at least noncommittal when the Stealth Zapper criticizes another teacher. Not only is it unprofessional to

Comments about colleagues should also be dealt with directly, if possible.

denigrate a colleague, but it also gives the Stealth Zapper ammunition to use at another time with another teacher. None of these teacher responses needs to be delivered in anything other than a conversational tone of voice. You just want to be sure the Stealth Zapper understands that you don't accept her implications about your colleagues.

> **Stealth Zapper:** I'm so glad Jimmy got you for a teacher instead of Mr. Golden. They say he's never prepared for class.
>
> **Teacher:** (*thinking about seeing Mr. Golden doing a crossword puzzle during his prep period*) Well, I hope Jimmy enjoys biology this year.

Notice that you are not defending Mr. Golden nor acknowledging the accuracy of the Zapper's statement. You are just focusing on your own interaction with this child. If you stick with this strategy, the parent will eventually get the message that you are not a person who engages in small talk with parents about colleagues.

No matter what you think of a colleague, you need to remain positive or at least noncommittal when the Stealth Zapper criticizes another teacher.

Here's another example:

> **Stealth Zapper:** What do you think of your new principal? He doesn't seem to like kids.
>
> **Teacher:** (*refusing to take the bait*) Actually, he's a great guy. The kids really like him.

Even if the parent has verbalized exactly what you think, too, remember that you are not required to respond to questions that are essentially inappropriate.

> **Stealth Zapper:** What do you think of your new principal? He doesn't seem to like kids.

Here are some possible responses:

> **Teacher:** I really haven't heard that.

Or:

> **Teacher:** I'd think you'd have to like kids to be a principal.

Or:

> **Teacher:** Being a principal is a tough job. You can't please everyone.

Or:

> **Teacher:** He's still new to the school and not everyone knows him yet.

Or:

> **Teacher:** If you think it's such an easy job, you ought to try it!

Okay, maybe not that last one.

What if the Stealth Zapper persists and asks you outright what you think of a colleague? Respond firmly:

> **Stealth Zapper:** Don't you think the administration should do something about Ms. Roberts? I can't believe the stories I hear about her outside of school!
>
> **Teacher:** Honestly, I never make comments about other teachers.

Then stick with that response.

The Stealth Zapper may surreptitiously complain to a supervisor about you or another teacher. This is when she becomes more dangerous than annoying. Here's an example of a typical phone call:

> **Stealth Zapper:** This is Ms. Zapper. My son Kevin is in Mr. Jackson's biology class.
>
> **Principal:** What can I do for you, Ms. Zapper?
>
> **Stealth Zapper:** I hate to complain, but Mr. Jackson's last test was completely unfair.
>
> **Principal:** In what way?
>
> **Stealth Zapper:** Mr. Jackson had things on that test that he'd never even covered. Just about everyone in the class failed it.
>
> **Principal:** I'll look into it.
>
> **Stealth Zapper:** There is one other thing. I don't want you to use my name. I'm afraid if Mr. Jackson knows I've complained, he'll take it out on Kevin.

With some principals, this move is very effective. These are the principals who were absent when they handed out personal courage in principal training. These principals will actually bring up this issue with the teacher and refuse to divulge the name of the complainer. This administrative behavior is not only patently unfair to the teacher but is also guaranteed to make the principal the hot topic in the faculty room the next day. By agreeing to the Stealth Zapper's terms, he implicitly concurs that Mr. Jackson *would* take it out on poor Kevin.

An effective principal would handle the Stealth Zapper more like this:

Stealth Zapper: There is one other thing. I don't want you to use my name. I'm afraid if Mr. Jackson knows I've complained, he'll take it out on Kevin.

Principal: I'm sorry. If you're unwilling to let me use your name, there's nothing I can do about this.

Stealth Zapper: I can't believe that you refuse to investigate this issue!

Principal: I'm sure Mr. Jackson would want to know if Kevin had a problem with his test. Perhaps the best thing would be for you to set up an appointment with Mr. Jackson yourself to discuss it.

Stealth Zapper: I'll have to think about it.

> *The Stealth Zapper may surreptitiously complain to a supervisor about you or another teacher. This is when she becomes more dangerous than annoying.*

Teachers have a right to know if a parent has a concern, and which parent it is—not so they can take it out on the student, but so that they can judge whether or not the source is credible. It is easy for a parent to impugn a teacher to the principal, who will probably not know the students as well as the teacher and thus be less able to judge the validity of the complaint.

Principals and other supervisors need to insist that complaints from parents about grades or homework go directly to the teacher first. It's the professional way of handling a concern and shows respect for the teacher. If your principal doesn't insist on this rule for ordinary complaints, you can sometimes politely and respectfully suggest that course of action:

Principal: One of your parents complained about your test.

Teacher: Really? Who?

Principal: I can't really say.

Teacher: Because you don't know?

Principal: No, I know who it is. I just promised her I wouldn't tell you who it is.

Teacher: Because then she'd have to kill you?

Okay, say that only if you know for sure that the principal has a sense of humor, and you won't get fired. If there's even the slightest doubt about either of those issues, try something like this instead:

Teacher: It's hard to respond to that kind of criticism when you don't know who the student is.

Principal: Well, the parent said the test was on material you didn't cover.

Teacher: Which questions? What material? Which test?

Principal: I really don't know.

Teacher: You know, maybe the parent should just call and talk to me. It's impossible to respond or give you any information if I don't know the specifics.

Principal: She doesn't want to talk to you.

Teacher: Because . . . ?

Principal: Uh . . . she thinks you'll take it out on her child.

Teacher: You're kidding.

Principal: Look, I'll tell her she has to call you.

> *Principals and other supervisors need to insist that complaints from parents about grades or homework go directly to the teacher first.*

It may not go exactly like that, but eventually the principal will realize he's on shaky ground. If not, try this:

Principal: She doesn't want to talk to you.

Teacher: Well, that's too bad because it's easy to lodge an anonymous complaint. I really can't respond to something like that.

Principal: Did you give a test recently?

Teacher: Yes, I did. But the grades ranged from 54 to 100, so I really don't know what the issue is.

Principal: I'll get back to you.

Although you still may not find out who made the complaint, at least you will have made your position clear—that you cannot respond to anonymous complaints.

When dealing with the Stealth Zapper, remember these tips:

- Be careful of appearing to accept her insinuations, especially about colleagues. If you consistently refute or refuse to respond to her innuendoes, she will eventually stop using them.
- If you are the target of an anonymous complaint, refuse to accept the premise of the complaint until you explore where it came from. Explain to the principal or supervisor that it is impossible to know what exactly the parent means unless you know who the student is.
- Don't spend any more time with the Stealth Zapper than is absolutely necessary. It's too hard to keep your guard up for an extended period of time.
- Don't be lulled into a false sense of intimacy with the Zapper. She will often volunteer for school projects or field trips, and she can make herself invaluable that way. However, keep in mind that she is a parent, not a buddy, and keep your conversation professional. Don't even think of accepting her invitation to lunch, for example.

The Stealth Zapper's real agenda is sometimes obvious, sometimes not. Whether she uses flattery or criticism, her goal is to achieve some kind of advantage for her child.

One Stealth Zapper I knew was effusive in her praise of the band director, making a point of telling the principal how lucky the school was to have him on staff. When the principal passed the compliment along, the band director laughed. "Last year when her son didn't make first chair, she didn't have a single good thing to say about me," he said. "This year, when her daughter wants to be drum major, I'm wonderful. I'm the same guy I was last year. Go figure."

If you are the target of an anonymous complaint, refuse to accept the premise of the complaint until you explore where it came from.

Chapter 9
The Uncivil Libertarian

We know that students do not shed their rights at the schoolhouse door. Nor should they. But do these rights include passionate embraces, obscene messages on shirts, the F-word in its many forms, hazing, bullying, fighting, and visible underwear? Most teachers and administrators think not. The Uncivil Libertarian, however, fights for what he insists is his child's inalienable right to any or all of these.

I'm pretty sure that wearing pants around the knees is not a right our forefathers and foremothers died to protect, but you wouldn't know it to listen to some parents:

Parent: Wearing low pants is the style.

Teacher: We don't need to see Andrew's boxers.

Parent: It's just the style.

Teacher: He can dress however he wants off campus.

Parent: He's just expressing his individuality! It's his right!

What is interesting to me is that when I see the same student working at the mall at his part-time job, he is wearing the uniform of the Fast Food

Army, pants pulled up around his waist and maybe even belted. Kids don't seem to mind repressing their individuality for a few hours while they ask if you want fries with that. And they aren't taking your order with their hands in the back pocket of their girlfriend's jeans, either.

Defending a student's fashion choices is one thing, but some parents will even defend behaviors that suggest more serious problems later on:

Parent: It's not my son's fault if the little boy gave him his lunch money.

Teacher: Your son bullied the boy into handing it over.

Parent: They're friends.

Teacher: Your son is in sixth grade, and the other boy is a second grader.

Parent: Are you saying my son is a bully?

Teacher: Not at all. He's an extortionist. An incipient thug. A Soprano in training.

All right, all right—don't say that. You may *think* it, though, and hope that it doesn't appear in a little bubble above your head. Instead, try something like this:

Parent: Are you saying my son is a bully?

Teacher: I'm saying that a sixth grader shouldn't be taking a second grader's lunch money. And yes, intimidation falls under our antibullying policy.

By the way, when it comes to bullying, we need to make our position loud and clear:

Teacher: I've asked you to meet with me, Mr. and Mrs. Reardon, because we need to work together to keep your son from bullying other kids.

Parent: Richard isn't a bully.

Teacher: Here are some of the things I've had to address with Richard over the last week: calling another student a "faggot," pushing another student in line, putting another student up against the wall, and referring to our special education students as "retards."

Parent: Well, there is such a thing as free speech. And Richard was held back a year, so he's bigger than the other kids. It could just be he's clumsy.

Teacher: (*ignoring the "free speech" argument*) Name calling isn't being clumsy. It's bullying.

Parent: Okay, we'll talk.

Teacher: I'm glad to hear that. Because according to our school policy on bullying, Richard has already been warned.

Ah, another great side effect of retaining kids for an entire year! Anyway, the point is, we need to attend to bullying when we see it and not let kids or parents off the hook whatever they say.

Here's another example of the Uncivil Libertarian defending another of his child's rights—this time, underage drinking:

Parent: So Emily was drinking on the senior trip. Big deal. That's what the trip is for.

Advisor: That is not what the trip is for.

Parent: Oh, come on. You know they all drink.

Advisor: Kids and parents signed an agreement before the kids left. The agreement specifically stated that drinking was prohibited.

Parent: That's not a legal document. You really can't hold anyone to that.

The Uncivil Libertarian may think that he is protecting his child when he defends bad behavior, but, in fact, he places his child in an untenable position between the two major authorities in his young life—his parent and his teacher. In addition, he sends a message that somehow the child's bad behavior will be tolerated by the rest of the world when he grows up.

> *While children, especially adolescents, are constantly testing their limits, they want to know what the rules are and who's in charge.*

Although children, especially adolescents, are constantly testing their limits, they want to know what the rules are and who's in charge. They may not like the rules, but they still want them. In my experience, when a parent is rude to his child's teacher or principal in the child's presence, it doesn't make the child feel good—even if the child was rude just an hour or so before and that's the reason for the parent-teacher conversation in the first place.

The Uncivil Libertarian is often more difficult to deal with than his children, who by and large are fairly clear about the rules and how the system works. Students may not like the outcomes of their actions, but rarely are they surprised by them. Although it is gratifying to a student that her parent will defend her, she really doesn't want her parent to look foolish in front of the teacher. It's sometimes beneficial to have the student sit in the conference with the parent. In the following conversation, the student's presence helps clarify the situation:

Parent: So you're saying my daughter cheated on this assignment.

Teacher: Instead of doing her own work, she copied and pasted paragraphs from a reference website.

Parent: She probably didn't know she wasn't supposed to do that.

Teacher: (*to student*) Keisha, did you know you weren't supposed to do that?

Keisha: Not really.

Teacher: Were you in class when we went to the computer lab and talked about this very thing?

Keisha: Yeah, but I didn't understand it.

Teacher: You didn't understand that you needed to do your own work?

Keisha: Other kids did the same thing.

Teacher: We're talking about you here. I don't accept this work from any student.

Parent: She wouldn't have done it if she had known.

Teacher: Keisha knows that if she had done the same thing by hand—copying other people's words directly out of a book and handing it in as her own—it would be wrong. Am I right, Keisha?

Keisha: Well, yeah, but this is different.

Teacher: The only difference is that you did it on the computer.

Parent: This technology is all so new. Kids may have a hard time seeing the difference.

Teacher: It is different from when you or I went to school. The technology isn't really new to kids, though. They have grown up with it.

Parent: I'm beginning to see what you mean. Do you, Keisha?

Keisha: Yeah.

This is where the teacher should stop—just make the point and get out. Remember "deliver the message"? No confessions are necessary. You don't need to symbolically tie the student to a chair under a single light bulb and grill her. Keisha and her parent know what she has done, and they know it wasn't acceptable. It's time to move on to the problem-solving phase:

> *The Uncivil Libertarian is often more difficult to deal with than his children, who by and large are fairly clear about the rules and how the system works.*

Teacher: I'm willing to let Keisha do the assignment over.
Parent: Okay, fine. When exactly will it be due?

The major problem with the Uncivil Libertarian is his imperfect understanding of what constitutes a student's right. He often confuses "right" with "want." He is one of the most difficult parents to deal with because reason rarely works. He is convinced that you are trying to take away some perceived right, and his response to that injustice is often anger, as in the following example.

Parent: I want Buddy to be able to go on the Outdoors Club overnight trip to the nature center.
Teacher: The school rules are clear. Buddy was suspended for fighting, so he can't go.
Parent: He's been looking forward to this for weeks! He has a right to go.
Teacher: Participation in the overnight is not a right.
Parent: Well, I'd like to know how you can take something like this away from him when he really wants to go.
Teacher: I'm not taking it away. He's the one who got himself suspended.
Parent: It was the other kid's fault.
Teacher: I don't have anything to do with that. I just know Buddy can't go.
Parent: You haven't heard the last of this!

The teacher is left shaking her head. She may not be happy either. The timing is awful, and she knows Buddy would have enjoyed the trip. However, the rules about participation in extracurricular activities are clear. She didn't make the rules, but she is required to follow them.

While we are on the topic of angry parents, this is a good time to talk about setting limits in dealing with aggressive parents. Under no circumstances should a teacher respond in kind to a parent who has gone over the line. No yelling, swearing, or—God forbid—threatening to hit someone. However, when you have exhausted all of your professional resources, it's time to say, "Hasta la vista."

Suppose the meeting with Buddy's dad had gone like this:

Parent: Buddy is going on the overnight, and you can't stop him.

Teacher: Actually, I know that if Buddy is suspended, he can't go.

Parent: You could take him if you wanted.

Teacher: Actually, I can't.

Parent: (*shouting*) I am sick and tired of listening to this garbage! If you were any kind of a teacher, you'd take him!

Teacher: You'll need to take this up with the administration. I'm finished here.

When a parent becomes at all abusive or out-of-control, it's time to end the conversation. Here's another example:

Parent: Who do you think you are, failing Kelly?

Teacher: I didn't fail her. She refused to do the work.

Parent: Kelly may lose her scholarship because of you.

Teacher: It's not because of me. It's because of her.

Parent: You're the teacher. It's your fault.

Teacher: You were kept well aware of the situation.

Parent: If you weren't such a jerk, you would have passed her!

Teacher: (*rising*) This conversation is over.

You need to be polite, calm, and tolerant . . . up to a point. No one expects you to take personal abuse. When any parent begins a personal attack, it's time to end the conference. Future conferences, if any, should be held in the principal's office with the principal in attendance.

Here are the points to remember when dealing with an Uncivil Libertarian:

- Parents sometimes need to be educated regarding why a student's behavior is not acceptable. They still may not accept your reasons for your decisions, but you may assuage their anger when they understand the situation a little better.

Under no circumstances should a teacher respond in kind to a parent who has gone over the line.

- Try to be conciliatory, but still insist that the rules or school standards apply, whether or not the parent agrees with them.
- When parents become abusive or insulting, stop the conversation immediately. You may want to suggest that they take their concerns to the administration.

The Uncivil Libertarian unwittingly suggests a sense of entitlement to his child. It is a disservice to the child. The world outside of school simply won't buy it.

Remember "deliver the message"?
No confessions are necessary.

Chapter 10

Mr. NBA

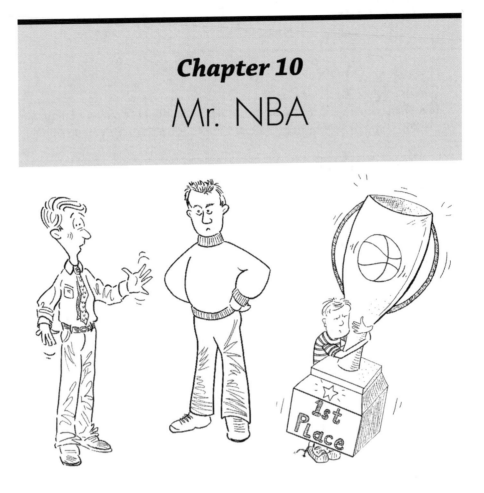

The percentage of kids who actually end up playing professional sports is tiny. Less than 1%. But to listen to some parents talk, you would think that their son or daughter is destined for the Hall of Fame in whatever sport he or she plays. The only obstacle, according to the parent (Mr. NBA), is that you, as the coach, don't seem to see all of the amazing potential the player has and don't give him or her the playing time, starting position, position on the field, or whatever it takes to win that full-ride scholarship to a Division I school.

From my experience, working with parents of student athletes could be a book in itself, so we're just going to touch on some of the more common behaviors and attitudes that can make things tough not only for the coach but for the player as well. Most kids do not want their father or mother to talk to the coach about their play, and all kids are embarrassed or even ashamed when a parent gets out of hand as a spectator. Still, some parents insist on being their child's biggest fan in ways that can make their child cringe.

Mr. NBA: Hey, Coach, I want to talk to you about Samantha's playing time.

Coach: Not now.

Mr. NBA: She needs more playing time. She's the best player you have!

Coach: Call me on Monday, and we'll talk. I can't talk to you during the game.

Mr. NBA: It's half time.

Coach: Now is not the time. Call me on Monday.

Most coaches I've known have learned from experience that it's best not to talk to parents during a game. Many coaches would agree that it's also a good idea not to talk to parents immediately after a game as well unless it's a big win, and everyone is congratulating the coach and the team. Even then, it's risky because emotions run high right after the game, and parents are most likely to be angry, upset, or frustrated about something that happened during the game—even if the team won. Coaches know it's better to wait until the following school day, when the parent has had a chance to calm down, before allowing him to scrutinize your coaching choices and tell you what you should have done. It doesn't guarantee a civil discussion, but it will improve your chances of having one.

When the discussion does occur, try hard to keep it focused on the parent's child and not on other players:

Mr. NBA: I think that Scott deserves more playing time.

Coach: I try to give as many players as I can time on the court, but we're still trying to win the game.

Mr. NBA: Scott has a better outside shot than Ray and plays better defense.

Coach: I've told Scott that I'd like to see him step up his inside game. And he needs to improve his free throw percentage.

Mr. NBA: No kid works harder than my son.

Coach: Everybody on the team works hard. I'm hoping Scott earns more playing time as the season continues.

When a coach meets with a parent, it's important that the coach doesn't say anything to the parent that he hasn't already said to the player. Notice in the example above that the coach says, "I've told Scott" [already] to step up his inside game." Sharing information or insights with a parent when you haven't already shared them with the player can be seen by the player as a betrayal of the coach-player relationship.

One parent I dealt with as a high school administrator was unable to convince her daughter's coach to give her more playing time, so she decided to harass the other players *on her daughter's team* from the stands with the hope that the coach would substitute her daughter for one of the other players once she pointed out their mistakes. Luckily for the players (and the coach), the principal was on it!

Mrs. NBA: What a poor pass, Number 6! You stink! Hey, Number 3, you can't shoot!

Principal: (*scrambling up into the bleachers to sit beside her*) We don't allow people to yell at players like that.

Mrs. NBA: You stink, Number 6!

Principal: You need to stop that, or you'll have to leave.

Mrs. NBA: Hey, I'm a taxpayer and a fan. I have a right to yell at anybody I want. Hey, Number 6! You can't shoot either!

Principal: Stop or you'll have to leave.

Mrs. NBA: You can't make me leave.

Principal: Do you want to follow me out, or shall I get the officer to escort you?

Actually, I love high school basketball, but because it's inside in the winter when people are bored and looking for a little excitement, it's always a little precarious, especially when there are long-term rivalries between schools. Most of the time things are fine, however, especially if all kids understand their own school's expectations of good sportsmanship and if the visiting team brings along one of their own school administrators. Still, there's always the parent who decides to moon the official after a bad call, or the parent who shouts a sexual slur at an official, or the parent who chest butts an official at the end of the game, or the parent who gets a golf club out of her trunk to threaten an official. Maybe you've never seen these exact behaviors at your school, but perhaps you've seen something similar!

Many coaches meet with the parents of their players before the season begins to go over the athletic policy and the sportsmanlike conduct expected of both players and fans. Although these meetings don't ensure exemplary behavior, they provide fair warning if it turns out that the coach or district officials have to restrain or remove a stubbornly intransigent parent from a game.

Student eligibility can be another hot-button issue for some parents. The school's athletic policy may affirm that student athletes must remain in good academic standing in all of their courses in order to be eligible to compete or even practice with the team. This is a policy that nearly everyone agrees with at the beginning of the year, but enthusiasm can wane as the season progresses.

Mr. NBA: You can't keep my son from playing just because he's failing Spanish.

Coach: The athletic policy clearly states that student athletes must be passing all of their courses in order to play.

Mr. NBA: He's doesn't need Spanish. He wants to play football at Ohio State, not Mexico!

Coach: Those are the rules. We talked about them at the parents' meeting at the beginning of the season. I sent the policy home.

Mr. NBA: I'm going to see his Spanish teacher!

Coach: You can talk to his Spanish teacher, but maybe you ought to talk to your son. I'm not happy about this either, but he needs to get his grade up.

Supporting the Spanish teacher is the best thing the coach can do even if it means a key player rides the bench while he learns to habla español. This is sometimes tough for coaches to do, but they need to remember that it's school policy, and it's their professional duty to adhere to it—even if it means losing a top player for a few games.

Still, we need to remember that all kids make mistakes, and that's why it's a good idea to have a clear athletic code that is shared with parents and is not too draconian. Many schools, for example, allow a student to continue to practice with a team while he works on getting his grades up. Some kids will stay in school only because of sports, and parents who don't plan on sports being their child's ticket to college may decide to make a child quit the team to punish him or her for poor grades or some serious error. This can be a mistake on the part of the parents, for they may unwittingly take away a tool that will help the child eventually succeed. Not every parent is Mr. NBA (thank heaven!), but some may actually undervalue the role that sports can play for some kids:

Parent: David is going to have to quit the team so he can bring up his math grade.

Coach: David really loves playing, and he's an asset to the team.

Parent: Baseball isn't going to get him into college.

Coach: You're right. But it's one of the reasons he's in school every day. Would you mind if I talked with him? Maybe we can work out a plan.

Parent: You can try. But if the grade doesn't improve, he's done.

Coach: We'll work on it.

Another issue that often arises with parents of student-athletes can be a little tricky from the coach's point of view:

Parent: My daughter's a senior. She should get to start and so should all of the other seniors.

Coach: Starting positions are earned.

Parent: It's not right that seniors sit on the bench while sophomores play.

Coach: At the varsity level, we try to win games. So we play according to skill, not year in school.

Parent: It breaks my heart to watch her sit there. It's not right.

Coach: I'm sorry, but that's the way we do it.

Parent: Your way shows a lack of concern for kids. It's not all about winning.

Coach: Your daughter is a solid player and contributes to the team.

Parent: But you won't start her.

Coach: No, not at this time. But if her game improves, maybe later.

Coaches need to be aware of how hard it is for parents of seniors, even parents who are generally supportive, to watch their child sit on the bench their last year while younger players start. And coaches need to keep in mind that while varsity sports are mainly about winning, all school sports are still about kids, the vast majority of whom won't even play college sports, let alone play professionally. So it helps to put kids in when the game isn't in jeopardy.

Sports are an important part of school, and coaches have a huge influence on kids' self-esteem and character. Maybe no kid from your school has ever played or will ever play professional sports, but kids can learn a lot about fairness, hard work, and teamwork through sports. We want them to participate. So coaches should keep in mind the following points:

- Don't talk to parents about their child before, during, or immediately after the heat of battle.
- Inform students and parents before the season begins about the athletic code and behavioral expectations for players and fans.
- Be sure that you have an athletic code and that it's up to date.
- Play as many kids as you can without putting the game in jeopardy.
- Remind parents (and yourself, on occasion) that it's not the NBA.

Sports should enhance a student's school experience just as other extracurricular activities do. But student participation is a privilege, not a right, and parents may occasionally need a gentle reminder of that fact.

Chapter 11
No Show's Dad

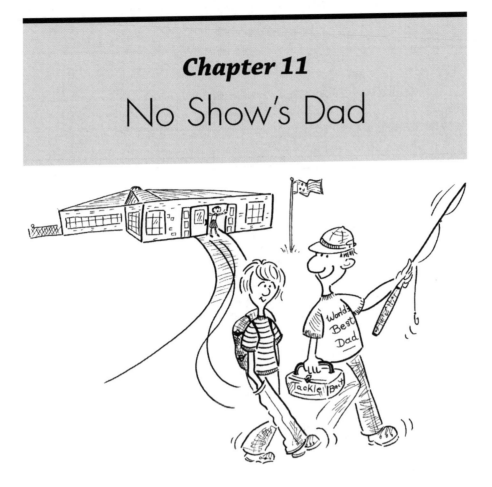

One truism about school is that you must be present to win. Although being in school every day doesn't guarantee that a student will graduate with honors, not being in school increases the chances that the student won't graduate at all. One kind of parent seems to think that attendance isn't mandatory, but optional—as if going to school is something to do if there's nothing else going on. Here is a typical conversation with a parent we'll call No Show's Dad:

No Show's Dad: We're taking Pete out of school for 2 weeks in March for a family vacation.

Teacher: You're taking him out while school is in session?

No Show's Dad: It's a lot cheaper to fly in March than later during spring break in April when everyone goes.

Teacher: He's going to miss 2 weeks of school!

No Show's Dad: That's why I'm telling you early. I'd like you to get all of his work ready for him in advance so he can take it with him on vacation.

There's also this example, a more common variation of the above conversation:

No Show's Dad: Just so you know, we're leaving a few days early for spring break, and we'll be back a few days late.

Teacher: Spring break is 5 days. How many days exactly will your daughter miss school?

No Show's Dad: Ten. But we're figuring that not much happens right before spring break and not much happens the first few days that kids are back at school.

Teacher: We'll be getting ready for state tests that are given 2 weeks after spring break.

No Show's Dad: No problem. She'll be back in time for the tests. And maybe you could give her some stuff to review while we're traveling.

It's hard to tell which is more annoying: That the parent thinks that missing a week or two of school is no big deal or that besides preparing materials for the entire class, you've got time to prepare additional materials for the student going on vacation.

This request for materials is difficult for a teacher. Although she really doesn't have time to prepare materials in advance for individual children, she also doesn't want to give the impression that 2 weeks of class time can be made up by completing a couple of assignments. She also knows that even if she does take the time to prepare special assignments, it's unlikely that the child will spend his time at Disney World working on his homework.

> *It is difficult for the teacher to prevent absences when they occur with the full consent (or even encouragement) of the parent.*

Still, no teacher wants to look as if she's unwilling to assist a child who really has no vote in the parent's decision. Nor does she want to appear punitive. In cases like this, it's usually best, despite her annoyance, to provide what she can that is readily available.

No Show's Dad: So I'm letting you know that we're going to be gone so that you can get all Pete's work ready for him in advance, and he can take it with him on vacation.

Teacher: (*thinking*) Fat chance. (*aloud*) I really don't think I'll have time to prepare special materials for your child ahead of time. I do have some study guides prepared in advance, and he can take those with him along with the class novel. He'll miss all of the math instruction, but maybe you can help him with some of the problems we'll be working on in class.

Note that it's not a bad idea to give parents some of the responsibility for tutoring or making sure work is completed.

While chronic absenteeism is a problem at all levels, it is particularly a problem at the elementary level when kids are learning basic skills.

Taking students out of class for an extended period of time is (thankfully) not too common. More often a student will be absent in smaller increments. Here's an example of another kind of conversation with No Show's Dad:

No Show's Dad: For Mitzi's birthday, we always take her shopping and then out to lunch.

Teacher: That sounds like fun. Her birthday is this weekend?

No Show's Dad: No, it's next Tuesday. So she'll be absent that day.

We know that the great majority of parents know better than to allow their child to miss school for frivolous reasons. But some seem to think that it doesn't matter what time the student arrives or what time he leaves, as long as he's spent some time in the classroom that day.

No Show's Dad: Sorry we're late. I just can't get Jenny to eat breakfast, and the result is that she missed the bus again.

Teacher: We do have breakfast at school every morning.

No Show's Dad: I know, but she'd rather eat at home.

Teacher: Maybe she'd just rather you drive her to school.

No Show's Dad: Well, it's not a problem for me, and she's only a few minutes late.

Teacher: She's a few minutes late about three times a week. I wonder if it would help to get her up a few minutes early.

No Show's Dad: Maybe. But she'll just dawdle anyway.

Teacher: It seems like you're the dawdler.

You know the drill. Think it, but don't say it.

At the middle school and high school level, there are often attendance rules regarding student-athletes. Some parents, although familiar with the rules, may have the mistaken belief that they don't apply to their child:

No Show's Dad: I know there's a rule about having to be on time for school if a student expects to play in the game that night, but it was my fault Sam overslept. I just didn't wake him up on time.

Coach: Sorry. He can't play.

No Show's Dad: But it wasn't his fault!

Coach: Sam is 17. He knows that he needs to get up.

No Show's Dad: I don't see why my son is being penalized for something that was my fault.

Coach: I'm sorry. He needs to be in school on time if he wants to play.

No Show's Dad: This is just not acceptable.

Coach: Sorry. That's the rule.

No Show's Dad: I'm going to the principal.

Coach: You need to do what you think is right.

Over the years, I've seen children taken out of school to get their ears pierced, to take care of siblings, to go shopping, to get their hair cut, to have lunch at a nice restaurant, to pick out a dog at the shelter, and to pick out a prom dress at the mall. Of course, to be fair, I've also seen kids come to school with earaches, fevers, and spots. Maybe it all evens out, but I doubt it.

It is difficult for the teacher to prevent absences when they occur with the full consent (or even encouragement) of the parent. Making it even more difficult for the teacher is that if she confronts the student about a suspicious absence, No Show's Dad will blithely supply a legitimate excuse for the child's not being there. Getting a pedicure can morph into "having a dentist appointment," or going to opening day at the ballpark may become "running a fever." In the spirit of full disclosure, I went to a number of opening days myself in my youth. The difference was that while my parents allowed me to go, they refused to write a note excusing my absence, and it never occurred to them or to me that they would lie about where I was.

> *When a child is chronically absent for no legitimate reason, some parents will look for other excuses for the child's lack of progress.*

The best a teacher can do when a child is chronically absent or tardy for nonlegitimate reasons is to hold the child accountable for work missed. The teacher should insist that the child make up assignments, and she should call the parents to solicit their support. Should a parent fail to cooperate, I suggest that the teacher keep a log of those calls and the parent's response. If you send a progress report home noting the child's absences as well, ask that the parent sign it and send it back. Some parents may need to be reminded of a teacher's previous efforts when the report card comes out.

> *A welcoming attitude on the teacher's part is particularly important for some unfortunate kids who have had to move many times during their school years.*

Although chronic absenteeism is a problem at all levels, it is particularly worrisome at the elementary level when kids are learning basic skills. At the elementary level, parents can sometimes be overprotective, keeping a child home if she complains of the mildest of upset tummies. At the high school level, on the other hand, parents are sometimes underprotective, turning their heads to ignore frequent truancy.

When a child is chronically absent for no legitimate reason, some parents will look for other excuses for the child's lack of progress:

Parent: I'd like you to refer my child for testing. I think he has a learning disability.

Teacher: I can do that, but he's missed so many days this year that it will be hard to get a clear assessment.

Parent: He just hasn't made the progress he should.

Teacher: He's missed 45 days. Perhaps the problem is attendance.

Parent: Or maybe he's got a learning disability.

Teacher: Maybe, but I haven't seen any evidence of that. I'd like to see how he does when he's here every day. I think that would make a huge difference.

Parent: I know my rights. I want my child tested.

Teacher: I'll have the school psychologist mail you the consent forms.

This area is a delicate one for teachers. Federal law gives parents the right to have their child tested, and the teacher certainly doesn't want to be seen as an obstacle in this regard. There is also a real possibility that, although the teacher doesn't recognize a disability, it may still exist.

Still, it *is* hard to guess how a child would have progressed if he had actually been in school. As long as you respect the parent's rights, it doesn't hurt to raise the question of the child's attendance being part of the problem.

It's tough for a teacher to change parents' attitudes toward attendance. That doesn't mean you should stop trying:

Teacher: I'm worried about Patrick's attendance. He really needs to be here.

Parent: Well, he's had a little cold.

Teacher: It's going around, I know. But he missed some important instruction. He really needs to be here.

Parent: I'll try to help him catch up.

Teacher: That's good, but he really needs to be here.

It's the old broken record technique: He really needs to be here. He really needs to be here. He really needs to be here.

When a parent is honest about a child's absence, it usually makes things a lot easier—unless he thinks that honesty gives the child a free pass:

Parent: I admit that Bobby skipped school last Friday to go to the beach with his friends.

Principal: I appreciate your honesty.

Parent: Well, unlike some parents, I'm not going to lie and say he had a dentist appointment or something like that.

Principal: As I said, I appreciate that.

Parent: So I don't think he should have a penalty.

Principal: Well, he still skipped school. He missed his group presentation.

Parent: Can't he do it at another time?

Teacher: It was a group presentation.

Parent: So he gets a zero? This is what we get for being honest?

It's a dilemma. You want to reward honesty, but you also know that the reason being honest is laudable is that the person is willing to take the consequences. After all, if all a person had to do to escape punishment was to "fess up," our prisons would be empty.

However, the parent is not going to want to debate philosophy. The best course of action is generally to try to find some kind of reasonable compromise:

Parent: Penalizing my kid for honesty isn't fair.

Teacher: I understand how you could feel that way. Your son tells the truth and gets a penalty while it appears that other kids get off scot-free. But he did skip. So if he's willing to write a 2-page report, I'll count it as his group presentation.

Parent: Well, I'm not happy about it, but I guess it will have to work.

Teacher: Well, I'm not happy about giving up my time to grade another assignment. And I didn't get to go to the beach either.

Okay, you know the drill about that last comment.

Despite all of the negative consequences of missing school, teachers really have little control over attendance. We can encourage kids to come to school, and we can talk to their parents and try to impress upon them how important regular attendance is to the child's success. In the end, however, we can't control what the parent does unless the absences become excessive enough to turn the problem over to the legal authorities.

What you can do as teaching professionals, however, is this: When the child who is chronically absent finally does show up at school, welcome him with open arms. You may be annoyed and frustrated that he has been absent for no real reason; after all, the absence creates work for you, he doesn't have the materials, he isn't up to speed, etc. However, giving the student a hard time only exacerbates the problem. Why would he want to come back if it's going to be unpleasant? So show him all of the good things he's missing at school!

A welcoming attitude on the teacher's part is particularly important for some unfortunate kids who, through no fault of their own, have had to move many times during their school years. I have known children who have been in four or five schools before they get to middle school. One family I knew enrolled the children every fall, then went south for the winter and enrolled them in school there. In the spring, the family returned to the North and re-enrolled the children in the original school. Needless to say, few kids can handle with aplomb that kind of peripatetic life, so we don't want to add to the problem. When they're in your classroom, even if it is just a pit stop, make it a warm and safe experience.

Parents who take kids out of school when they don't really have to do so send the message that school isn't as important as teachers would have them believe. We need

> *When they're in your classroom, even if it is just a pit stop, make it a warm and safe experience.*

to help them remember that 50% of success in life is showing up. The remaining 50% is effort. We need to work at making kids want to come to school because they don't want to miss anything, and we need to tell parents over and over what their child won't get to do or see or read or participate in when he isn't at school. One way we can do that is to communicate frequently with parents of absent children either by phone or weekly updates. It's a little additional effort, but it may pay off for the child.

Here are some ideas to keep in mind when dealing with No Show's Dad:

- If he asks for his child's work ahead of time, give him what you can and suggest how he might tutor the child while he is away.
- Do everything you can to educate No Show's Dad about how much the child misses when he's not in school.
- If attendance in school is required for participation in an extracurricular activity, stay the course. No Show's Dad needs to know that classroom attendance is a prerequisite for other activities.
- Point out how chronic absenteeism can negatively affect a child's progress, but be prepared to assist the parent who wants a referral for psychological or other testing.
- When a chronically absent child does appear, make her feel welcome and part of the class. Showing annoyance or ignoring the child only reinforces reasons not to come to school.

Of course, the most important thing you can do to encourage students to come to school is to make your classroom inviting and your lessons interesting and challenging. You can't *make* students come to school, but you can help make it a place where they feel wanted and welcome.

Chapter 12
The Advocate

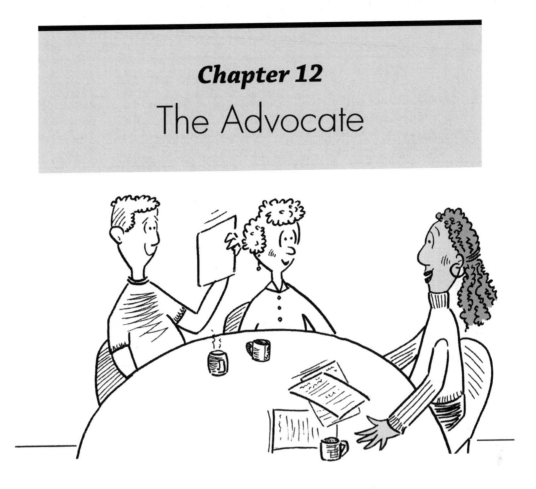

Some difficult parents are born that way; others are made. Parents of special needs kids often fall into the latter category. They don't necessarily start out being difficult, but if they find themselves having to frequently advocate for their child with school people unwilling to acknowledge and provide for a child's special needs, they can become difficult and demanding. Of course, some parents of special education students, like any parents, might be difficult in any situation, but we need to keep in mind that it's not a contest between the teacher and the parent when the child's learning is at stake. For example:

Parent: I want my child tested immediately!

Teacher: I'll need you to fill out the paperwork giving permission for the school psychologist to test him.

Parent: I just gave you my permission.

Teacher: We need to have signed permission.

Parent: Fine. But I want it done tomorrow.

Teacher: I know the school psychologist has lots of requests for testing. She will let you know when she can schedule it.

Parent: I'm not happy about the delay. We need to find out what why my child is having learning problems.

Teacher: His record shows that his teacher last year recommended him for testing. And it looks like his teacher 2 years ago did too. At that time, you didn't want him tested.

Parent: Things weren't as bad then.

Teacher: Okay, let's get this paperwork signed, and we'll get things moving.

Some parents of special needs students can become frustrated and disappointed in their child's progress and that frustration can spill over in meetings:

Parent: John needs to have a 1:1 aide in the regular classroom with him at all times.

Teacher: Actually, that isn't on his IEP. (*IEP stands for Individualized Education Program, an educational plan that provides accommodations and other arrangements for children with special needs.*)

Parent: How can you expect him to make progress without an aide?

Teacher: I think John has made excellent progress this year on the modified curriculum.

Parent: If he had an aide, the curriculum wouldn't have to be modified.

Teacher: You should address your concern with the committee. I don't have any authority to approve an aide.

Parent: The committee won't approve it either. How is he supposed to learn anything?

Teachers have the responsibility to read the IEP for every student in their class who has one. The responsibility is both professional and ethical. Teachers need to be aware of any modifications that the child is entitled to, and they need to adjust their classroom procedures and requirements accordingly, remembering that not only are they required to do so by law, but that modifications are in the best interests of the child.

But another important reason that teachers should be familiar with a child's IEP is so they know what's *not* required. Some parents will press for additional

Teachers who are well aware of a child's special needs and requirements and follow through accordingly have a greater chance of working well with the child's parents.

modifications that are not part of the child's IEP. Sometimes

So it's not easy for the classroom teacher to meet the needs of all of her students all of the time, but it's not for lack of trying!

those requests don't present a problem; they are minor and don't require a great deal of effort on the part of the teacher. For example:

Parent: I'd like Alana to be seated in the front row so she will be less distracted.

Teacher: That's not a problem. We can make that work.

Here's another example:

Parent: If Mark can just hang on to his squeezy ball, it helps him calm himself.

Teacher: As long as he's not tossing it to or at his classmates, no problem.

But on occasion a parent will ask for a modification that is not stated in the child's IEP. For example:

Parent: John needs to have more time to finish his tests than the other students.

Teacher: That testing modification is not in his IEP.

Parent: Can't you just do it anyway?

Teacher: I don't have a problem with giving him extended time. I suggest you get in touch with the school psychologist and ask to meet with the committee to add extended time to his IEP.

Changing a student's testing modifications may not seem like a big deal to you as the teacher, but you need to remember that changes to a student's IEP are made by the committee on special education or child study team (or whatever the group is called in your state), not by individual teachers.

Teachers who are well aware of a child's special needs and requirements and follow through accordingly have a greater chance of working well with the child's parents. And when you are present at a special education meeting with the child's parents, school officials, and maybe the child himself, you want to be sure that you are conversant about the child's classroom needs and have thought about what you want to say about the child's progress. There are few things that frustrate parents more than a teacher who seems unfamiliar with the child's IEP and has not made the required adjustments.

Having said that, sometimes even when a teacher has done all she can to help a special needs child progress, some parents may still be unhappy. When this situation occurs, school people should not allow them to become abusive or threatening any more than they would allow any parents to behave that way. To be perfectly candid, I have seen school people in special education meetings sometimes allow parents of special needs children to behave in ways that would be considered unacceptable with parents of children in regular education. Allowing uncivil behavior does not improve the child's education and may in fact encourage the parent's behavior to become a habit. Instead, all school people should insist on civility; if that is not possible, the meeting should conclude and perhaps be rescheduled. For example:

Parent: I don't agree with the testing results you've shown. I want an independent test.

School psychologist: I believe the results we're showing are valid.

Parent: I'm having my son tested independently. And you people are going to pay for it. It's pretty clear to me that you don't know what you're doing.

School psychologist: Well, we do know what we're doing. It may be that you just don't agree with the results.

Parent: You people are idiots.

School psychologist: This meeting is over.

On the other end of the spectrum, parents of gifted students can sometimes be particularly demanding. For example:

Parent: What special learning projects do you have planned for Emily?

Teacher: We really haven't been in school long enough for me to get to know Emily's interests.

Parent: Emily has an IQ of 138. I expect to see some enrichment activities that challenge her this year.

Teacher: There are several students in this class who will enjoy doing special projects. I should be able to get some things organized for them in a few weeks.

Parent: I hope so, and I'll be checking in occasionally. She's very, very bright, and she needs to be challenged.

Teacher: I'm sure we can find some things here in first grade she'll like.

Parents may not always understand that a classroom teacher may have a very wide range of abilities and needs in her class, especially if her school has a strong

Teachers who are responsive to their student's individual needs often turn difficult parents into supportive parents.

inclusion program. An elementary classroom of 25, for example, may contain students who are hearing impaired, learning disabled, physically handicapped, and gifted or who have autism or ADHD—along with students of average ability. In addition, some students may be gifted and learning disabled or physically handicapped with high ability, and students who have generally average ability may be particularly capable in math but less so in writing or art. So it's not easy for the classroom teacher to meet the needs of all of her students all of the time, but it's not for lack of trying!

Still, here's a conversation you don't ever want to have with the parents of a special needs child:

Parent: According to John's 504 plan, he's supposed to get a copy of your worksheet a couple of days early so he has time to do it before class.

Teacher: I didn't know John had a 504 plan. Is that like an IEP?

Some teachers may be unaware that a student has a 504 plan or that the plan is a legal document that may require a teacher to make small modifications to the student's learning plan. You will want to be familiar with both 504s and IEPs that your students may have. Parents are much more impressed (and the student will have a better chance at making progress) if the conversation goes something like this:

Parent: According to John's 504 plan, he's supposed to get a copy of your worksheet a couple of days early.

Teacher: I haven't handed any worksheets out yet, but I'll be sure that John has his early according to his plan.

So here are a few tips to keep in mind when working with the Advocates:
- Remember that aggressive advocates are sometimes made, not born, after trying to work within a system that they may perceive as unresponsive.
- Read and be familiar with your students' IEPs and 504 plans. Make any modifications required by those documents.

- Recognize that while it's tempting to always teach to the middle, students on both ends of the spectrum deserve the same opportunities to learn.
- Take the time to be well prepared for special education meetings with specific examples of the student's progress.

Teachers who are responsive to their student's individual needs often turn difficult parents into supportive parents. We need to keep in mind that we're all really on the same side—the child's side.

Chapter 13
Helicopter Mom

True story: Several years ago, a big football game was scheduled between two long-standing rivals. Not only was it Senior Night for the home team, but the outcome of the game would decide the league championship. Unfortunately, it had been raining for days, and the home team's football field had turned into a shallow lake. The opponents offered the use of their field, which had better drainage and was in better shape, but the home team's superintendent was loath to lose the home field advantage.

Instead, the superintendent, a former military man, called in a favor from a nearby army base. That afternoon a couple of helicopters arrived and hovered low over the field, the chopper blades whisking the standing water away from the ball field. The game was played, the home team won, and the superintendent and his helicopters became the stuff of local legend. It was glorious.

"Glorious" is not the word I would use to describe another kind of helicopter—the parent who hovers constantly, ready to whisk away any problem or inconvenience that might befall her child. The Helicopter Mom is heavily invested in every facet of her child's school day. Here's a typical conversation:

Helicopter Mom: Sorry to call you so late, Mrs. Baker, but we're not sure if Ian's homework is page 37, the odd problems, or page 36, the even problems.

Teacher: What? It's 11:00 at night!

Helicopter Mom: Just so you know, Ian's already asleep. I'm just checking his work for tomorrow.

Teacher: Checking? Or doing?

I know, it seems unlikely that Ian will be getting up at 5 a.m. tomorrow to complete his homework, which, by the way, you had on the board and gave your students time to get started on at the end of class. Still, your last comment should be:

Teacher: As I wrote on the board, it's page 37, even problems. Good night.

Helicopter Mom begins hovering when her child is in kindergarten and never lands on anyone but school people. Sometimes she actually starts much earlier, preschool or even sooner, hovering over the crib with flash cards while a mobile tinkles Mozart above the baby's head.

She is always at her child's beck and call, providing her elementary school child with a cell phone, ready to intervene at any moment. Miss the bus on Monday? Mom will drive you to school. Miss the bus on Tuesday, Wednesday, Thursday, and Friday? Hop in the car. Forget your violin? Mom will deliver it to the main office before orchestra meets. Lose your gym shoes? Mom will get you another pair tonight. Fail the math test? It probably wasn't fair. Talk back to the teacher? You didn't really mean it.

> *Helicopter Mom begins hovering when her child is in kindergarten and never lets up.*

Helicopter Mom spends a lot of time at the school or on the phone. She questions the teacher about his grading practices. She challenges the pronunciation of words at the spelling bee. She interrogates the principal about the dress code. She wonders whether children should go outside for recess if the temperature drops. She calls at the first snowflake to see if school is going to close early. She yells at the referee. She challenges the superintendent about graduation honors. Eventually, she fills out her child's college applications and drafts his college essay. It doesn't take long for the child to get the lay of the land:

Helicopter Mom has a very hard time letting her child take responsibility for his actions

> **Teacher:** Mark, that language is not acceptable in my classroom. I'll see you after school.
>
> **Mark:** I need to call my mom first to see if it's okay.

Or:

> **Teacher:** Christine, your answer is right, but you didn't show your work.
>
> **Christine:** My mom helped me on my homework last night. She said it's okay not to show my work if I could do it in my head.
>
> **Teacher:** It's great that your mom helped you, but I need to see the work.
>
> **Christine:** My mom said it didn't matter.

Or:

> **Helicopter Mom:** Alan has soccer practice every night after school, so he's not going to get his health project in until next Monday.
>
> **Teacher:** The projects are due on Friday.
>
> **Helicopter Mom:** I don't want Alan getting stressed out over this.
>
> **Teacher:** Well, I don't either, but the students have had more than a week to complete this project.
>
> **Helicopter Mom:** Don't worry. He'll have it on Monday.
>
> **Teacher:** I'm not worried. But if it's handed in past the due date, he'll lose points.
>
> **Helicopter Mom:** I just don't think that's fair.
>
> **Teacher:** I'm sorry. But I need to apply the grading procedures equally to all of my students.
>
> **Helicopter Mom:** It's too bad you can't be more flexible.

Helicopter Mom has a very hard time letting her child take responsibility for his actions:

> **Helicopter Mom:** I brought this for Mark's lunch.
>
> **Secretary:** I think he has in-school suspension today.
>
> **Helicopter Mom:** I know that. I thought a McDonald's Happy Meal would cheer him up.

> *It isn't easy for the teacher to put responsibility back on the student, but that's where it belongs.*

There is a difference, of course, between parents who are simply interested and involved in their child's school and parents who need to know everything that's going on so that they can shepherd their child through each day and every class, protecting her from any real responsibility. Helicopter Mom is likely to make demands on the teacher, rather than on her child:

Teacher: Amy is not handing in all of her homework.

Helicopter Mom: I'd like you to send home a daily report about what she's turned in and what she still needs to do.

Teacher: I have 135 students. I can't promise to do that.

Helicopter Mom: I would think that would be part of your job.

It isn't easy for the teacher to put responsibility back on the student, but that's where it belongs:

Teacher: With 135 students, I can't promise you that I'd be able to send home a daily report.

Helicopter Mom: How am I supposed to know if Amy does her work then?

Teacher: You could ask Amy when she gets home to show you her homework.

Parent: She always says she's already done it.

Teacher: How about if she writes down the assignment every day in her plan book, and I'll initial it? You can check when she gets home to see what her assignment is.

Helicopter Mom: How will that help?

Teacher: Well, I suggest that along with her plan book, you insist that she bring her math book home every day. You can check the assignment and ask her to show you her work.

A favorite Helicopter Mom ploy to help a child avoid consequences is to insist that the child didn't know what was expected. He didn't know when the paper was due. He didn't know he needed to use three sources for the research. He didn't know he needed a title page. He didn't know he needed to do his own work. He didn't know the project was half of his final grade. All of these excuses will make the teacher want to ask what the child *does* know, besides how to manipulate his mother.

Often, what Helicopter Mom really wants to show is that every problem is really the teacher's fault because he didn't tell the child. Here's an all-too-common conversation:

Helicopter Mom: Alana didn't know the test was going to be Friday.
Teacher: I reminded students daily, and it was on the board all week.
Helicopter Mom: She doesn't always look at the board.
Teacher: I sent the information home in my weekly update.
Helicopter Mom: She must have forgotten to give it to me.
Teacher: Well, that's unfortunate, but there isn't much more I can do besides telephone you every day right after class.
Helicopter Mom: That would be great!
Teacher: (*startled*) I'm joking.

Oops. The teacher forgot the "no sarcasm" rule, but you can see how that could happen.

Other excuses Helicopter Mom uses for her child is that the work is too hard, the assignments too long, or the test too difficult. The teacher needs to reassure her that he knows the child, and he is confident that the child is capable of doing what is assigned. The teacher should add that he has the same expectations of all of the other students as well. Here is an example of one way to handle Helicopter Mom:

Helicopter Mom: I really think that 25 pages of reading a night are too much.
Teacher: Students have time to begin in class.
Helicopter Mom: Brad just can't stay awake to finish it. Besides, he needs to have a little time to relax and play on the computer.
Teacher: Brad is a bright boy. He can do this. Of course, I expect the same from him as from other students.
Helicopter Mom: I just don't want him to become discouraged with school.
Teacher: He's a pretty positive kid. And I know that kids need to have time to relax and do something else besides schoolwork. It's not easy to balance

On the other end of the spectrum, some Helicopter Moms fret over things that most other parents don't even notice, and as a consequence, can put a great deal of pressure on their kids.

99

everything. But maybe he can play on the computer after he does his reading—sort of as a reward.

Helicopter Mom: I don't see that as a reward. He deserves to have some downtime.

Teacher: How many pages a night do you think Brad can read?

Helicopter Mom: I have no idea. Not 25.

Teacher: How about if you monitor his reading for a week. Let me know what he can accomplish in half an hour. We have quite a bit of reading to get through this semester, and students need to organize their time to stay on top of it.

On the other end of the spectrum, some Helicopter Moms fret over things that most other parents don't even notice, and as a consequence, can put a great deal of pressure on their kids:

Helicopter Mom: I see Madeline's math grade dropped 3 points.

Teacher: She still has a 94 in math.

Helicopter Mom: What did she miss?

Teacher: Actually, I'm not really sure. There were a lot of assignments and quizzes over the last marking period.

Helicopter Mom: Can she do something for extra credit?

Teacher: She got a 94!

Helicopter Mom: Maybe we should get her a tutor.

Teacher: Maybe you should get a life.

Well, by now you know the teacher shouldn't really say that. He should say something like this, instead:

Teacher: Let's wait and see how she does over the next few weeks. Madeline's an excellent student and a lot of fun to teach. Grades tend to fluctuate a little for all students, so I really think she'll be fine. If not, I'll let you know.

Helicopter Mom: Okay. But please call me as soon as there's a problem.

Besides an abiding interest in her own child's progress, Helicopter Mom sometimes has a similar interest in the progress of other students. Protecting her own child means making sure that no other child has an unfair advantage. In conversations like this one, it is important not to acknowledge her point:

Helicopter Mom: My daughter's written work is a lot better than Oren's.

Teacher: I have a policy not to talk about other children.

Helicopter Mom: Well, I'm just saying that Nan should get the writing award at sixth-grade graduation. I've seen Oren's work, and I know that Nan's is better.

Teacher: Nan is a very good writer.

Helicopter Mom: I'd say the best in the class.

Teacher: She is very good—as are several of the other students.

Here's another example:

Helicopter Mom: I see Bella got a perfect attendance award. Why didn't my Lewis get one?

Teacher: Ahhh . . . Lewis didn't have perfect attendance.

Helicopter Mom: He was only absent twice this year.

Teacher: Well, perfect means being here every day.

Helicopter Mom: I know for a fact that Bella's mother brings her to school even when she's sick. Lewis was out 2 days because he caught a cold from her.

Teacher: Really, there's no way of knowing exactly who gives whom a cold.

Helicopter Mom: I saw Bella in the nurse's office, coughing and sneezing when I came to pick up Lewis one day.

Teacher: Really, I can't comment on that. I'm sorry, but perfect attendance means just that. The child has to be here every day.

Helicopter Mom: Well, I just think it's not fair.

If it isn't your policy not to talk about other students, it should be. Professional ethics demand that you respect the privacy of all of your students. Helicopter Mom can be insistent, and you have to adhere to your ethical position. Here's one approach:

Helicopter Mom: Beth says that the reason she did poorly on the test is that you spend all your time helping Larry. Isn't he one of those "special" kids?

Besides an abiding interest in her own child's progress, Helicopter Mom sometimes has a similar interest in the progress of other students.

Teacher: I'm sorry. I can't talk about other students.

Helicopter Mom: Well, I don't know why those kids are in regular classes. It takes the teacher's time away from the other students.

Teacher: Really, I just don't talk about other students.

Helicopter Mom: It doesn't seem fair to the rest of the kids.

Teacher: Beth didn't do well on the test because she missed a couple of days and didn't come in for extra help.

Helicopter Mom: Well, if you weren't so busy with those special kids, you could have helped her in class.

Teacher: All kids are special.

You get the picture. Refuse to be drawn into any comparison between or among your students.

Helicopter Mom often loves to volunteer at school. Although having parent volunteers usually works out wonderfully for both the parent and the school, teachers need to be alert when Helicopter Mom is involved. She may find it difficult not to interfere on her child's behalf—as in chastising a first grader who won't sit next to her child at lunch. Or she may not respect another child's right to privacy, telling tales out of school about a child who may have had a problem of some sort in school that day.

If you have parent volunteers in your classroom, never, never allow them to grade papers or enter information into a grade book or other kind of record. Doing so compromises the confidentiality of your classroom. And never share personal information about another child in your classroom with a parent volunteer.

In dealing with Helicopter Mom, the best defense is a good offense. Keep her informed of her child's progress, by phone, e-mail, snail mail, or conference. Many schools today even have online programs that allow parents 24-hour access to their child's grades and assignments. Regular communication makes it hard for a student or her parents to claim ignorance. By the same token, failing to inform a parent of a problem will indeed make it your problem—and rightly so. Keeping parents informed when their child is not being successful is part of our professional duty.

Helicopter Mom can be trying to a teacher, but think of how trying she also must be to a child struggling to balance roots and wings. It is Helicopter Mom's lack of perspec-

If it is not your policy not to talk about other students, it should be.

tive that gets her into trouble. The teacher's job is to help establish and then maintain a sense of perspective for her.

Here are some strategies to remember when dealing with Helicopter Mom:

- Reassure her that her child is capable and can compete with the other students in the classroom.
- Communicate with her as clearly and frequently as possible.
- Insist that her child play by the same rules as all of the other children.
- Keep to yourself confidential information about her child and other children.
- Rejoice that at least she cares about her child!

Chapter 14
The Competitor

With the Competitor, every encounter with the teacher is a contest. She enters your classroom like a WWE wrestler or a Transformer climbing into the ring. She's already pumped up and eager to fight for what she wants. She makes it clear that if she gets her way, she wins and you lose. She approaches every situation as if it were a serious competition that will probably end in a smackdown. You will be the one lying flat out in the middle of the ring, unless you know how to handle her.

As teachers, we know that working with kids is not about winning and losing. We know that teaching is not about who's right. We know that working with parents should be a cooperative effort, not a competition. We struggle to remain professional, but a confrontational parent can press every one of our buttons. It isn't long before the idea of winning becomes pretty appealing to us as well. Here's a typical conversation:

Competitor: Your writing program isn't very effective.

Teacher: Why do you say that?

Competitor: I did a little research yesterday on the Internet.

Teacher: (*thinking*) And I did a little research in my 5 years of college. (*aloud*) So what did you find?

Competitor: Here, I've printed it off for you. You can read it later. This study shows that kids can move more easily from printing to writing if you use the Gutenberg method instead of the method you use.

Teacher: Thanks, I'll look it over.

Competitor: Great. I'll call you in a couple of days about changing the writing program.

Teacher: I don't think we'll be changing the writing program.

Competitor: We'll see . . .

Here's another example:

Competitor: In the last school we were in, the teachers and kids all made piñatas for the last day of class before the holidays.

Teacher: How nice.

Competitor: I want to do that here. It would be fun.

Teacher: It *would* be fun. Maybe we could do something like that next year.

Competitor: There's no reason not to do it this year.

Teacher: Actually, it's only 2 weeks until vacation, and we have other things planned.

Competitor: I'll get some mothers to help. Kids need to have fun in school.

Teacher: I agree—about the fun. But we won't have time for that this year.

Competitor: I'm sure you can find just an hour for fun. Let's plan on it.

Teacher: Every day is fun. (*thinking*) Except for today.

The Competitor does not like to be wrong. She also doesn't like for you to be right. She will not hesitate to point out the error of your ways:

Competitor: I rechecked Michael's math test, and you graded one of the problems wrong.

Teacher: I did?

The Competitor does not like to be wrong.

It can't be a competition if you refuse to compete.

Competitor: Yes. He had it right, and you marked it wrong.

Teacher: Let me see. Hmm. Yes, I think I did miss one.

Competitor: So you were wrong, not Michael.

The Competitors do not like to admit mistakes themselves. If they have not been successful with their child in some areas, they may not want you to be either because it makes them look bad:

Teacher: Waldo needs to stay with me after school to make up work he didn't do.

Competitor: He'll never do that.

Teacher: Then he'll fail.

Competitor: You're letting him fail?

Teacher: I'm giving him the opportunity to do the work.

Competitor: He won't stay.

Teacher: You can't make him stay?

Competitor: You can't either.

These kinds of exchanges can be maddening. However, you need to keep in mind that it can't be a competition if you refuse to compete:

Teacher: Waldo needs to stay with me after school to make up work he didn't do.

Competitor: He'll never do that.

Teacher: Can you help me get him to stay?

Competitor: Look, he's a big kid now. He makes his own decisions.

Teacher: Maybe you would have more success making him stay than I would.

Competitor: Me?

Teacher: Well, I can't seem to do it. You're his dad. I'll bet you would have more success with Waldo than his teacher would.

Competitor: I doubt if he'll listen to me, either.

Teacher: Well, maybe I can get him to make up some work during his lunch period or study hall.

Competitor: Maybe. You could try it. And I can tell him that he should work with you during study hall.

Note what the teacher has done. He doesn't say what he's tempted to say, which is "Okay, forget it. If you don't care, why should I?" Instead of pushing against the parent, the teacher pulls him over to his side.

The Competitor is taken off guard when you refuse to play the win-lose game. Admittedly, it often isn't easy to think win-win with her. She may challenge you in the classroom, on the phone, or via e-mail or text, trying your patience and testing your cool. It is helpful to remember, however, that the hostility aimed at you is sometimes a result of her own frustrations with the child. This misdirected frustration can come across as something else—bravado, disrespect, or anger toward the teacher.

> *The Competitor is taken off guard when you refuse to play the win-lose game.*

Here is an example of a conversation that is going nowhere fast:

Competitor: Why is my son staying in when all of the other kids go out for recess?

Teacher: Kids who haven't finished their work need to finish it before they can go out.

Competitor: I want him outside with the other kids.

Teacher: That's not the rule in third grade. Jimmy needs to learn to finish his work.

Competitor: I do not want him staying in. He needs to go out and play with everyone else.

Teacher: He can go out when he finishes his work.

Clearly, if the teacher lets Jimmy go out without finishing his work, he loses. The teacher, that is. Well, Jimmy does, too. So how do you keep the parent from "winning"?

Think win-win. What does the parent really want? First of all, he probably doesn't want his child to be stigmatized or embarrassed by being the only one stuck inside the classroom on a glorious fall afternoon. In truth, no parent would want that—nor would you if it were your child. It is important to realize that what the parent really wants is for his kid to do his work like all of the other kids. Going outside is unlikely to be the real issue. Sometimes a teacher needs to hear what isn't being said.

In a case like this, it is probably a good idea for the teacher to figure out another plan to help Jimmy get his work done—one that involves the parent's help. Otherwise, the parent will focus on the side issue (playtime) instead of the main issue (Jimmy's failure to do his work).

Teacher: I don't like to see kids miss playtime, especially Jimmy. He needs to work off some of that energy. But there's only so much time in the school day and you know how Jimmy procrastinates. Do you have any suggestions to help him get his work done?

Competitor: Not really. You're the teacher.

Teacher: When he doesn't get his work done, he falls behind in class. Third grade is an important year. I worry about his progress in reading comprehension, and I know you do, too.

Competitor: I do worry about that. But he still needs his playtime.

Teacher: How about a compromise? He gets 10 minutes of playtime after 10 minutes of homework.

Competitor: Well, I guess we could start there.

Of course, this particular solution won't work for all cases. The point is simply that if there is going to be any kind of reasonable solution, it will probably fall to the teacher to work out some kind of compromise. If the teacher can acknowledge some validity in a parent's concern, she can open a dialogue that at least has a chance of ending with a positive outcome.

Here's another example of a conversation with the Competitor:

> *If the teacher can acknowledge some validity in a parent's concern, she can open a dialogue that at least has a chance of ending with a positive outcome*

Competitor: Alyssa is being bullied by Natalie, and it needs to stop immediately!

Teacher: I thought Alyssa and Natalie were best friends.

Competitor: They were. But since a new girl moved here, they're not anymore. You should know that.

Teacher: What does the bullying look like?

Competitor: They don't talk to her, and they whisper to one another about her. It needs to stop! This is happening in your classroom.

Teacher: I'll talk to them.

Competitor: Well, I'm holding you accountable. If it doesn't stop, I'll go to the principal.

Teacher: You need to do what you think is right. But just so you know, I realize that there is nothing more painful in seventh grade than the way girls sometimes treat one another. I'll work on it.

Competitor: I just hate to see Alyssa so unhappy.

Teacher: We need to find a way to solve this problem.

Finding a solution to the problem, however, often requires that the teacher ignore all of the implied criticisms the parent brings to the conversation, which is not an easy task. Again, if you can figure out what the parent really wants (and it's not always what the parent says), you may be able to find a way to work through the situation so that everyone wins, including the child.

Sometimes, however, what the parent says is exactly what she wants—but she just can't have it. Here's an example of when a teacher needs to hold her ground:

Competitor: When you call on Mary and she doesn't know the answer, it embarrasses her. So I want you to stop calling on her.

Teacher: Mary always has the option to pass.

Competitor: Then other kids will still think she doesn't know the answer.

Teacher: Other kids pass too.

Competitor: I'm telling you: I don't want you to call on her anymore.

Teacher: I'm sorry. That's part of the learning process and a quick way for me to find out if Mary understands the material. I will be calling on her.

Competitor: Then I guess I'll have to talk to the principal.

Teacher: Bring it on.

Okay, by now you know that's just a little joke. You should not say, "Bring it on." You should say, "Go for it."

No, not really. What you should really say (as we've noted before) is, "You need to do what you think is right."

Finally, on occasion, you will meet a Competitor who weirdly (and sadly) wants to compete with the teacher in criticizing the child. She wants to make sure that you don't even *think* about blaming her for her child's lack of progress. The results of her attitude sometimes end up with the parent and teacher changing places:

Competitor: The problem with Charles is that he's just plain lazy. Like his dad.

Teacher: I wouldn't call it laziness. I think he needs to get organized and keep a regular schedule.

Competitor: Well, I'd like to see you try to get that kid on a schedule.

Teacher: Does he have his own quiet place to study?

Competitor: He's not interested in studying.

Teacher: I think he wants to do better at school.

Competitor: I don't think he cares.

This is the worst kind of conversation with the Competitor because the teacher begins to suspect that she's given up on the child or that she has no control over his behavior. When this happens, the teacher's only choice is to take charge and ask for the parent's support as he suggests a plan for the student:

Competitor: I don't think he cares about school. I don't think you can make him.

Teacher: I'd like to try. Why don't the three of us meet—you and Charles and I? We can work out a study plan together. He can stay with me a couple of nights after school, and we can figure out a plan at home.

Competitor: I don't think it will work, but it's worth a try.

By this time the teacher is feeling a little sorry for Charles. Even if he *is* a little lazy!

Let's recap some of the suggestions for dealing with the Competitor:

- Refuse to be drawn into a competition that is likely to produce a winner and loser.
- Think win-win. How can you find a workable compromise? Look for common ground.
- Listen to what the parent is *not* saying. Ignore, if possible, the implied criticisms and focus on the real issue.
- Encourage the parent who has completely unreasonable demands to take them to the principal.

When you have managed to deal successfully with the Competitor, feel free to close your door, raise both arms, and do a victory lap around the desk.

Chapter 15
Who's the Fairest of Them All?

One year an eighth-grade boy who was driving me crazy complained to me about another teacher. "She always yells at me," he said.

"Mark," I chided him, "I yell at you, too."

"Yeah," he said, "but you yell at all of us. Not just me."

Point taken.

Every teacher has, at one time or another, a student who drives her to distraction. Mark was one of those kids. At parent conference time, I was a little anxious about meeting his parents, but they seemed pleasant enough when they arrived in my classroom.

I began my litany of Mark's offenses: He didn't do his homework, he wasn't always on time for class, he spoke without raising his hand, and he talked to other students when I was talking. One time he was showing off to his classmates about how he could fit into his locker, and they closed him inside. I heard the banging and let him out.

His parents shook their heads in commiseration. "Yes, he's a handful," his dad agreed. "But he's a good boy. And you're his favorite teacher."

"What?" I said. "I'm his favorite teacher? How can that be? I am on that boy's case from the beginning of class to the end!"

"Well," said his dad, "he says you're tough, but you're tough on everyone."

He meant that as a compliment. When I thought about it, I remembered that kids have a rich, innate sense of what is fair and what is not. It turns out that Mark was okay with my yelling at him because he wasn't the only one and because he knew it meant I cared about what he did. He didn't take it personally, and he was pretty sure I liked him, even if I wasn't always happy with his behavior, which he admitted, with typical eighth-grade candor, wasn't always exemplary. (Just for the record, I use "yell" in the sense of speaking loudly but sweetly!)

Good teaching demands fairness.

Good teaching demands fairness. This is an important point to remember not only from a professional ethics standpoint, but also from the standpoint of dealing with your students' parents. Difficult parents can be confrontational and demanding. If a teacher has actually been unfair to their child, they can be even more confrontational and demanding—and also right.

We need to make every effort to treat all children the way we would want our own child's teacher to treat her. Remember that every parent wants to know if his child is just another student to you, or whether you really know him. Parents want to know if they can count on you to treat their child fairly, even kindly. They hope that you see in their son or daughter all of the special things that they do.

If you are a parent as well as a teacher, you know exactly what I mean. If you're not a parent, think of a child you love—a niece or nephew, the kid next door, or even yourself as a child. Be the kind of teacher you wanted to have when you were a kid.

It's not easy to treat all kids equally because in the real world of teaching, you will not like all kids equally. After all, you don't like all adults equally, do you? The trick is that no one should ever be able to guess which child you like and which child you just can't warm up to. It is important to particularly monitor your behavior with kids you may find less than appealing, so that you can be sure that you treat all children equally.

If you are always fair, you may, on occasion, even find yourself with an opportunity to help a student whose behavior isn't particularly charming:

Charlie: You're the Honor Society advisor, right? So how come I didn't get in?

Ms. Anderson: Sit down, Charlie. Let's talk. Do you have any thoughts yourself?

Charlie: Teachers don't like me.

It's tempting for Ms. Anderson to say the following:

Ms. Anderson: Well duh! You're smart, but you're rude and lazy. Honor Society is about more than grades!

Instead, she acts like the professional she is—and that we should all hope to be:

Charlie: Teachers don't like me.

Ms. Anderson: Why do you say that?

Charlie: I don't know. They just don't.

Ms. Anderson: Can you give me an example of what you mean?

Charlie: Well, like Ms. Banks, my English teacher.

Ms. Anderson: Why would Ms. Banks not like you?

Charlie: I dunno. Well, there was that time I told her to f-off.

Ms. Anderson: Well, duh!

No, she doesn't really say that. She's a professional. She says this:

Ms. Anderson: Can you see how that might change how she thinks of you?

Charlie: Yeah.

Ms. Anderson: So what do you think you can do about it?

Charlie: Well, I guess I could watch what I say to her. But it's hard because she's always giving me a hard time.

Although this brief conversation won't change Charlie overnight, his teacher's willingness to talk to him about a real problem is a step in the right direction. We need to remember that for some kids, it's the adult guidance they get in school that makes a difference in their lives. We need to be careful that we don't lapse into an unproductive cycle: When a kid reacts negatively to our criticism or correction, we give him even more criticism and

And that is the hard part: in the real world of teaching, you will not like all children equally

correction. Instead we need to work hard to change patterns of behavior by developing both trust and mutual respect with our students.

Students recognize when they are not treated fairly. They also recognize when other students are not treated fairly. I have known teachers who thought they would ingratiate themselves with their students by making jokes at another student's expense. Although some kids laughed, the teacher lost respect in their eyes—because kids not only understand fairness; they also understand power. When a teacher picks on a student just because he can do so with impunity, it offends the students' sense of what's right. Kids may pick on one another themselves, but it's not the same as when the teacher does it.

When I was an elementary principal, I was passing an open computer classroom when I heard the teacher say sarcastically, "Boys and girls, Donald doesn't even understand how to cut and paste. That's because Donald doesn't pay attention, right, boys and girls? Donald is going to have a hard time on this assignment, boys and girls." That's when I appeared in the doorway and said, "Mrs. Brown is kind of mean, isn't she, boys and girls?" Okay, by this time you know I didn't say that, but I did say, "Mrs. Brown, please see me today when you have a moment." I left out the "boys and girls" part.

Why spend so much time on fairness? Here's why: Stuff happens in schools that we can't control. Therefore, it is very important to control what we can. Remember Helicopter Mom? We can't always predict what will make her decide to swoop in and land on us. But we can guarantee that she will be revving up her engines if you let one child retake a test on which she made a poor score but deny that privilege to her son. If you think Ms. "Quit Picking on My Kid!" is unreasonable, wait until you ignore foul language from one kid and remove her child from class for the same offense. And you really don't want to have to face the Intimidator after you've humiliated his child by pointing out to the child's classmates how he can't even tie his shoes. Of course, if the child who is humiliated is also a child with special needs, prepare to apologize in front of not only his parents, but perhaps the principal, the school psychologist, and other interested parties at a meeting. And then think about whether teaching is what you really want to do.

> *Kids may pick on one another themselves, but it's not the same thing when the teacher does it.*

We know that there's just no pleasing some people. However, we can conduct ourselves in a way that minimizes encounters with difficult parents by perfecting our skills, thinking before we act, and fine-tuning our sense of fairness in our interactions with our students.

As teachers, we all need to be critical of our own work. If not, others will be happy to do the job for us.

Chapter 16
Tips for Effective Parent Conferences

So it's parent-teacher conference time again, and you are completely prepared. You know that some parents will be intimidated or annoyed if you sit behind your desk while they sit like students in front of you. Therefore, you will meet with them at a table, or perhaps you will all be seated at student desks. You want to show that you are all on the same side.

You have examples of each student's work, as well as test results, organized in folders that you can immediately put your hands on. You may also have at your fingertips printed materials that explain your reading program, an upcoming project, or the state testing schedule.

You plan to start each conference on time and end promptly so that parents don't get backed up waiting to see you. You know which parents don't have the same surname as their child. You are dressed professionally, and you are not drinking coffee, a soda, or anything else that parents will not have access to.

In 98% of the meetings, both you and the parents will actually have an enjoyable time and feel as if you are working together for the benefit of the child.

Before you rise to greet your first parent and shake his or her hand, you remember what we said at the outset: All parents want to be reassured that you really know their child, that he or she is not just another student to you, and that you will do your best to help him or her learn. Parents may also want to know how their child is doing in comparison to other students; that is, is their child at the top of the class, somewhere in the middle, or lagging behind? If he isn't making adequate progress, is he getting the extra help he needs? Also, you will want to keep in mind that, particularly at the elementary and middle school levels, parents want to know how their child gets along with other children. You will be kind but candid.

In 98% of the meetings, both you and the parents will actually have an enjoyable time and will feel as if you are working together for the benefit of the child. You may even learn something about the child that you didn't know before and that might be helpful in your work with him or her.

Then there's the other 2% of meetings—those that may not be so enjoyable. Luckily, you will have reviewed some of the ideas and strategies we have talked about in this book, so you can go in with a plan for dealing with difficult parents. Some basic reminders:

- Be courteous even if it's a challenge.
- Remain professional.

In addition, keep in mind these strategies:

- Never, ever use sarcasm when speaking to parents, even if the parent is sarcastic. Sarcasm only inflames an already volatile situation and diminishes you as a professional:

  Parent: I suppose you think my child isn't smart enough to take advanced math.

  Teacher: It wouldn't take a genius to see that.

  Parent: (*climbing over the desk*) What?

- Be a broken record if necessary.

  Teacher: Jack's frequent absences are affecting his work.

  Parent: He spent last week at his dad's house.

Teacher: He's missed some important instruction.

Parent: His father lets him do what he wants.

Teacher: It's hard for him to get caught up when he's out so much.

Parent: His father lets him stay up too late and then he can't get up the next day.

Teacher: I'm hopeful that his attendance will improve, because it's going to affect his later work as well.

- Refuse to acknowledge anonymous complaints.

  Parent: I know for a fact that you favor the girls in your class.

  Teacher: How would you know that?

  Parent: I have my sources.

  Teacher: Really, I can't respond to that.

  Parent: Well, the kids know it. Even the girls say you favor them.

  Teacher: Kids say a lot of things. Let's talk about Connor's report card.

- Stay the course. Some things are not negotiable:

  Parent: Okay, Beth admits she cheated on the test. But I don't see why she can't just take it over.

  Teacher: She will get a zero for the test.

  Parent: Why can't she just take it again?

  Teacher: She is familiar with the test. I am offering that she write a paper instead to make up for the zero.

  Parent: That isn't fair. No one else has to write a paper.

  Teacher: No one else cheated on the test.

  Parent: She's not going to do it.

  Teacher: That's her choice. But the zero then stands.

- Encourage parents to make sure their children come to school and arrive on time. If parents themselves don't show up at conferences, make a phone call. And keep in mind that not every school schedules conferences at times that are convenient to parents. Some parents have to work; others may be responsible for childcare. So when you call, be as positive as possible:

  Teacher: I missed you at parent conferences last night.

Parent: I had to work.

Teacher: Well, I'm glad I caught you at home this morning. Trisha is doing pretty well in school and has made real progress in math, but she isn't doing her homework every day.

Parent: When I ask her if she's done it, she always says yes. And sometimes she says she doesn't have any.

Teacher: Just so you know, I give a little math homework every night. You can count on it. If she says she's already done it, maybe you could ask to see it.

Parent: I can do that.

Teacher: Trisha is really having a good year except for the home-work. Thanks so much for your help.

Parent: You're welcome. And I'll be checking on Trisha's math.

- Show parents how you are helping students build confidence through accomplishment. Focus first on what the child is able to do and how you plan to build upon the skills she already has. A good way of doing this is to contrast the student's work at the beginning of the year with where she is today:

  Teacher: Here's a sample of Rashida's writing last September. Look at what she can do now!

  Or:

  Teacher: Angelo has passed every quiz so far this year, so I can tell he's doing the work.

- Talk like you mean it. In other words, know what you're going to say before the conference so you can say it with conviction. Practice what you want to say if the conference involves giving parents information they may not want to hear. Be sensitive to parents' hopes and dreams for their child, but be direct enough so that parents are not confused about your message:

  Teacher: Steve has made progress in reading, but he's still not where he needs to be. He's about a year below grade level. That's why he has an extra reading class each day.

- Be sure you can justify your classroom rules or procedures as important for students rather than just
for your own convenience.

Parent: Can Sean stay with you on Tuesdays to
work on his multiplication tables?

Teacher: I usually drink coffee and play fantasy
football in the faculty room on Tuesdays.

> *Remember that if a parent becomes abusive or threatening, it's time to end the conference.*

Just wanted to see if you were still paying attention! Of course,
you don't say that (or do that). Here's what you say instead:

Teacher: I'll be here.

- Try not to take parent criticism personally, even when you're pretty
sure it is meant that way, and let parents vent if they have to. They
won't hear anything you say anyway until their particular issue is
resolved. Don't interrupt except to ask clarifying questions:

Teacher: Thank you for coming in. I'm interested in hearing your
concerns.

Parent: Well, it's about the play tryouts you had in class. Rachel never
gets a good part. She thought she had a chance at *Cinderella*, but
instead you picked Rebecca, who always gets the lead. Rachel
is just as good, maybe better, and last year when they did *Peter
Pan* she ended up being the dog, and Rebecca, as usual, got to be
Wendy.

Teacher: I see.

Parent: She came home and cried and cried. She doesn't want to be
an Ugly Stepsister. I mean, what girl would?

Teacher: Okay. Is there more?

Parent: Well, I just think that things should be spread around.
Rachel tries really hard and every time she loses out. Two years
ago she had to be a tree when Rebecca got to be a wood sprite.
It's just not fair.

Teacher: I see your point. Maybe we can find a part for Rachel in the
next play that allows her to do a little more.

> *Be sensitive to parents' hopes and dreams for their child, but be direct enough so that parents are not confused about your message.*

However this issue is resolved, it's clear that before Rachel's mom can talk about her daughter's progress in math, she needs to make it clear that in the next play Rachel shouldn't have to be a flying monkey while Rebecca gets to be Dorothy. Maybe the teacher has never thought about how something as simple as a school play can impact a child's feelings about herself or about school.

On the other hand, maybe the parent needs to know that Rachel is so shy and anxious that when she has to do an oral report the teacher worries that she'll faint and hit her head on the chalk tray. That information will take a little finesse on the teacher's part.

- Refuse to be intimidated. You are a trained professional who understands classroom management and child behavior. Remember that if a parent becomes abusive or threatening, it's time to end the conference:

  Parent: I expect to see an improvement in Terry's grade in Spanish.

  Teacher: Part of Terry's grade is participation in class. When he doesn't do the homework, he's not prepared to participate.

  Parent: That is the stupidest idea I've ever heard! How can you grade participation?

  Teacher: Students should be prepared to respond in Spanish to questions in class.

  Parent: This isn't the only course he has. But it's certainly the most useless course. And you're the most useless teacher.

  Teacher: *(standing)* This conference is over.

The great majority of parent conferences will be positive and useful. When they are not, you should have the strategies to make your points clear without exacerbating the situation. Sometimes, however, we just have to admit that we're not making any progress toward working with the parent for the benefit of the child. So in the next chapter, we'll talk about what to do when nothing works.

Chapter 17
When Nothing Works

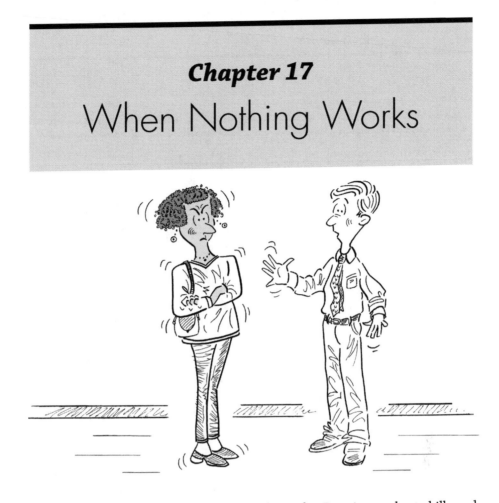

It's discouraging when nothing we do works. Despite our best skills and efforts, some parents will simply refuse to be cooperative and work with the teacher for their child's benefit. Whatever the reason, a very, very small minority of parents will resist all of our attempts to come to an amicable resolution to the problems they perceive. When you as the teacher have exhausted all of your strategies and maybe your patience, you may simply decide to politely and firmly put the cards on the table and bring negotiations to an end:

> **Teacher:** Mr. Barton, I think we're at an impasse. I cannot in good conscience change Brian's grade. You will need to take this problem to the principal.

Or:

> **Teacher:** Mrs. Chen, it seems that we cannot come to an agreement about what's best for your daughter. We may have to just live with the fact that this is the way I run my class. I know you're unhappy, but this is how I do it.

Or:

> **Teacher:** Mr. Samson, you cannot call me at home. You may call me at school and leave a message, and I will get back to you as soon as I can. But I will not call you more than once a week.

Or:

> **Teacher:** I recognize that we don't agree. But Amanda will have to be respectful in my class or she cannot stay. And you cannot show up in my classroom every time you disagree with my rules.

Or:

> **Teacher:** Ms. Lopez, please be aware that from now on I will not meet with you without the principal present.

These tactics will not necessarily make a demanding parent less demanding. However, you will have made it clear that there are limits to what any teaching professional should have to tolerate. From this point on, the parent will have to deal with the administration. (Of course, you will have kept the administration informed all along.)

From a districtwide perspective, the administration should insist on a "chain of command" approach to handling garden-variety parent complaints: teacher first, then principal, then various supervisors, then superintendent, then board of education. This philosophy can be shared with parents in newsletters and school handbooks, and school administrators can help by insisting that parents follow the chain of command with common problems. Although the teacher can't control how the district operates in this regard, she can frequently remind parents—in notes home, in phone calls, or in conferences—that if there is a problem, she wants to hear about it first.

Of course, there are circumstances that demand the principal's or even superintendent's immediate attention—serious incidents that involve a child's safety or well being. There are, unfortunately, occasions where a parent needs to move swiftly to the top to rectify a situation or remove his child from harm's way. But the usual kinds of classroom complaints that parents have—grades, homework, tests, assignments, behavior, attendance—should first be addressed with the teacher. The first

You will have made it clear that there are limits to what any teaching professional should have to tolerate.

question a principal should ask when a parent calls is, "Have you talked to the teacher?" Teachers can encourage principals to follow this process by saying something like, "I sure wish the parent had just talked to me first. It would have saved a lot of time and effort on your part."

If the issue remains unresolved, it's okay for concerned and/or dissatisfied parents to move on to the next level and the next and the next, up to and including the board of education or even the commissioner or state school board. It can be both costly and time consuming to move up the system, but some parents are willing to do it and sometimes it is absolutely the right thing to do.

Other times, it's stupid. But, hey, we can't control that.

Unlike some professionals, teachers generally do not have the benefit of selecting their clientele. With practice, though, teachers can develop their skills in interacting with parents so that, in the end, the child benefits. As a teacher, you may not have picked the child's parents to deal with, but neither did the child.

Focus on the 98% of parents who are supportive and reasonable, and develop the skills you need to withstand the other 2%. With a little practice, even the 2% can be tolerable if you keep your sense of humor. If you follow some of the suggestions we've talked about, someday you may even have this conversation:

Parent: I want to apologize for my behavior the other day. I was upset. You were right about what my son needs to do to be successful, and I will see that he does it.

Teacher: Thank you. I appreciate your apology.

Parent: To show how sorry I am, I'm going to pay off your college loans and start a campaign to increase teachers' salaries by 50%.

Ha ha. Just a little joke. What the parent really says is this:

Parent: But I still think he deserved an A!

Chapter 18
A Final Assessment

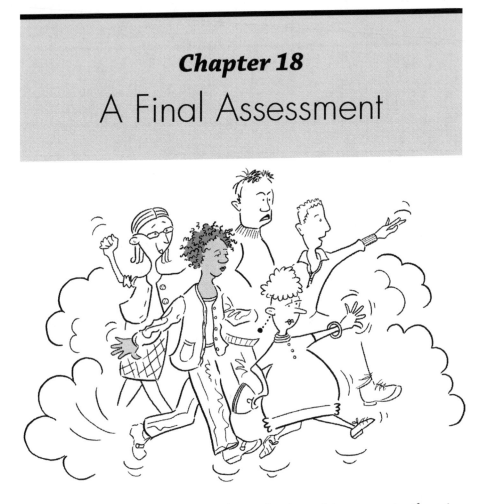

As we've pointed out earlier, this is the Age of Assessment—there is a test for everything. Let's see how well you do in picking out the teacher's correct conversational responses in the following situations.

ITEM #1

Parent: Jimmy brings a can of Sprite to school for lunch because he doesn't like milk.

Teacher: Well, the policy in our school cafeteria is that kids can have milk, water, or juice. We don't allow soft drinks.

Parent: What my child drinks is my business, not the school's.

What should the teacher say next?

a. Right. That's why your child weights 80 pounds in second grade.

b. How are those dental bills working out for you?

c. I'm going to ask our principal to give you a call to talk about this. When is a good time for you?

Answer: C. This is a school rule, not a classroom rule. Let your principal work with this parent (and maybe the school nurse too!).

ITEM #2

Parent: We're leaving for vacation 3 days early and coming back 3 days late. Will Tanya miss anything?

What's the best response?
a. Nope. Nothing. We're just going to hang out for those 6 days until she gets back.
b. Wait. Let me get this straight. You're taking your child out of school for 6 *days*, and you're wondering if she'll miss anything?
c. We'll be introducing a new unit in geometry. We'll be starting a new novel. And we'll be working on our science research projects.

Answer: C. The reason you will not respond with either A or B is that you remember the basic rule: No sarcasm. Instead, you will respond professionally with C. Of course, you know what's coming next:

Parent: Oh, okay. So could you get Tanya's work ready for her in advance so she won't get behind?

What's your response this time?
a. When pigs fly.
b. I'll do my best, but I may not be able to have all of the materials ready that far in advance.
c. Just tell her to take a book along to read.

Answer: B. We have already talked about why you won't respond with A. And although C is tempting, it gives the impression that Tanya really isn't going to miss anything important during the 6 days of class she will be gone. Despite your annoyance, do the best you can—and maybe add that she should take along a book to read anyway.

ITEM #3

Teacher: I wanted to talk to you about Orson. I'm worried that he has a tendency to bully other kids.

Parent: What proof do you have?

Teacher: I've had complaints from his classmates about his threatening to hurt them if they don't give him their pens or pencils or even their money for snacks.

Parent: I find that hard to believe. Orson is a good boy. I'd worry about other kids bullying him.

Where should the teacher go from here?

a. Look, I need your help on this. I've already spoken with Orson, and I need you to reinforce that he's going to find himself in real trouble if this behavior continues.

b. The kids have a nickname for him: The Enforcer.

c. Were you ever bullied yourself as a child?

Answer: We're going with A. You need to be clear with the parent that there will be serious consequences if Orson's behavior continues. The parent may deny to you that her child is capable of bullying but that doesn't mean she doesn't believe you.

ITEM #4

Parent: I hope you don't mind, but I brought you a little present.

Teacher: A present? Why?

Parent: You've been so kind to Jessica.

Teacher: Jessica is a good student. She's easy to teach.

Parent: Well, just to show our appreciation, we'd like you to have this gift certificate for one of the clothing stores downtown.

Teacher: (*opening the envelope*) It's for $200!

Parent: It's the least we can do for all you've done for Jessica. And I know she'll be asking you for a college reference pretty soon too.

What is the teacher's next response?

a. Really, I can't accept this.

b. Jessica is a great student. I'd be happy to write her a reference. You don't have to give me anything to do it. I just can't accept this.

c. Actually, could you exchange this for a certificate for the hardware store? We need a new water heater.

Answer: Don't even think about C. Okay, maybe think about it while you're taking a cold shower at home. The first thing you say is A, followed immediately by B. Never accept a gift worth more than a couple of dollars from a parent. Although some school districts prohibit gifts of any kind, most will allow the occasional coffee mug or plate of cookies at the holiday season. Never, ever accept a gift of alcohol (e.g., a nice bottle of wine) or cash. Acceptance of such gifts compromises you and the profession.

ITEM #5

Parent: I'd like you to move Melissa's seat.

Teacher: Why?

Parent: I don't want her next to that Williams kid after she got head lice from him last month.

Teacher: I'm not sure the school nurse determined where they came from.

Parent: Well, with that kid's home life, it's pretty clear. His mother doesn't take care of those kids, and everyone knows about the parties that go on in that house. The place is filthy. My daughter shouldn't have to be subjected to that kind of thing.

Teacher: Sitting next to Adam Williams doesn't subject Melissa to anything like that.

Parent: I want her moved.

What is the teacher's best response?

a. Look on the bright side: If your daughter has head lice it means she has friends.

b. I don't talk about other children or their families.

c. I have a new seating arrangement every few weeks so that kids can learn to work with lots of children.
d. I'll move Melissa.

Answer: Here's why you can't choose D: If you do, you tacitly admit that "the Williams kid" gave Melissa head lice. If Melissa shouldn't sit next to him, then neither should anyone else.

As most elementary teachers know, once you have a contagious illness or infection (or infestation) in class, it's pretty hard to determine where it started. The important thing is to alert parents immediately to its presence, and have the school nurse determine when infected children may safely return to school.

The correct answer is B. Remember, you respect confidentiality and don't talk to parents about other children and their families.

What about A? It's only funny if your child is not infected.

ITEM #6

Teacher: If Alex wants to remain in my class, he's got to get his head up off the desk, his feet out of the aisle, and the earbuds out of his ears.
Parent: I don't understand why you let him act that way.
Teacher: I don't let him act that way. That's why I threw him out of class yesterday.
Parent: How's he supposed to pass English when he's not in class?

What's the best response?
a. Are you kidding me? Do you have earbuds in your own ears?
b. You and I have got to work together. He needs this course to graduate.
c. Maybe you could come to class with him every day.

Actually, when I taught high school, I did have a mom come to class for a while, and the improvement in her son's behavior was amazing! However, not a lot of parents will be willing to do this. Instead, I recommend answer B. Then add, "You and I should meet together with Alex so he can see we're on the same page."

ITEM #7

Parent: Why does John have to do this assignment over?

Teacher: The assignment was to write an original story.

Parent: So?

Teacher: So John retold an episode of *Star Trek*.

Parent: That's impossible.

Teacher: Well, he changed the names, of course—Captain Kirk becomes Captain Dirk, Spock becomes Sprok—that sort of thing—but it's still a *Star Trek* episode.

Parent: I'd like to see proof of that. You haven't seen every *Star Trek* episode. How would you know?

Teacher: Well, you're right. I haven't seen them all. But as luck would have it, this happens to be one I have seen.

Parent: My son isn't writing anything over until I have proof. John, is this your work?

John: Yes, it is.

Parent: If he says it is, then it is. My son doesn't lie.

Unless the teacher knows Klingon, which would put an immediate end to the discussion, he'll have to choose from one of these responses:

a. I'm sorry we don't agree on this, but I'm going to insist that John redo the assignment and write an original story.

b. Okay, I'll see if I can go back through all the episodes of *Star Trek* until I can find it and prove it to you.

c. All kids lie at some point. Even yours.

Answer: I'm sure you realize that even if you think C is true, saying it will only inflame the situation. B is a poor choice because even if you had the time and energy to find the exact episode that was used, the parent still may not believe there is enough similarity to prove anything. Go with A. If the parent says, "Well, John isn't going to do it," you know what the next response is:

Teacher: Then he will get a zero for the assignment.

And you know what to say when the parent says, "I'm going to see the principal:"

Teacher: You need to do what you think is right.

ITEM #8

Teacher: Michael has lost his computer privileges because once again I found him at a site that is not appropriate for students.

Parent: Frankly, I have a problem with that.

Teacher: I'm glad to hear that. We can't block everything on our server, and sometimes students can get to places they shouldn't be.

Parent: No, you misunderstood. I have a problem with Mike losing his privileges.

Teacher: Mike was warned twice about accessing inappropriate sites. The third time he loses his privileges for a week.

Parent: I thought the school had automatic safeguards that prohibit kids from accessing certain sites.

Teacher: We do. But Mike is pretty computer savvy and manages to get around the school software program.

Parent: So basically the school doesn't have the right program.

What is the best response at this point?

a. Yeah, it's our fault.
b. Are you telling me you think it's okay for Mike to access those sites?
c. Mike knows the rules. He's off for a week.

Answer: C. However, you may want to try B before ending with C.

ITEM #9

Teacher: Glad you were able to come to the conference, Mr. Berman.

Parent: Call me Fred.

Teacher: Okay, Fred. Your daughter is failing history.

Parent: Call me Mr. Berman.

Teacher: Well, Mr. Berman, your daughter is still failing history.
Parent: Does she need it to graduate?
Teacher: Yes, she does.
Parent: Well, Nan, I think you have your work cut out.

Which is the teacher's best reply?
a.   Well, Fred, hang on to those graduation announcements.
b.   Well, Fred, I think your daughter has her work cut out.
c.   Well, Fred, I'm going to need your help.

Answer: Remember that we prefer that both teacher and parent use the appropriate respective titles, but if the parent uses your first name, you can use his. Otherwise it's an uneven playing field. The answer is C.

ITEM #10

Parent: Why did you take my son out the last quarter of the game?
Coach: I make the calls, and I decide what will give us our best chance to win.
Parent: But Brendon was having a great game!

What's the coach's best response?
a.   It's the coach's call.
b.   Call me on Monday if you want to talk about this.
c.   He needs to be more aggressive when it counts.

Answer: A, followed by B if the conversation continues. Coaches need to remember not to engage an angry parent right after a game when emotions are high. Answer C will only add to an emotional encounter and continue the discussion. In addition, the coach needs to have that discussion with his player before he has a conversation with the player's parent.

BONUS ITEM:

Parent: I'm sick and tired of you picking on my daughter.

Teacher: I'm not picking on her. But I cannot tolerate her disrespect.

Parent: She says you don't respect her.

Teacher: I respect all of my students. But I will not tolerate your daughter's language.

Parent: You know you don't like her. Other kids do the same thing, and you just pick on her.

Teacher: Other kids do not use that language in my class.

Parent: If you ever kick her out of class again, you're going to answer to me!

What is the best response?
a. This conference is over.

Answer: A.

I'm sure you did very well on the assessment. You know that working with difficult parents requires practice, common sense, and keeping your wits about you.

As you've probably realized by now, describing difficult parents as "types" is simply a way to talk about specific strategies a teacher can use in specific situations. Difficult parents are more alike than dissimilar in their demands on the teacher and their refusal to allow their child to take responsibility for his or her own actions. A Helicopter Mom can turn into a Caped Crusader overnight. The Stealth Zapper can double as the Uncivil Libertarian. What's important is not who's who but what skills and strategies we've developed to deal with difficult parents.

Good teaching is not easy. It never was. And it is likely that parents will become more, not less, demanding. Teachers need not only to develop strategies to deal with parents, but also to develop a habit of reflecting upon their own teaching behaviors to avoid unnecessary conflicts.

When parents and teachers work together, their partnership benefits the child. Despite occasional conflict, helping a child be successful in school is the common goal for both home and school.

References

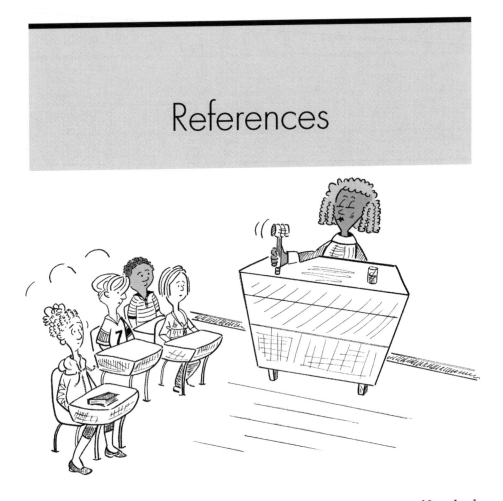

National Education Association. (2010). *Status of the American public school teacher, 2005–2006*. Retrieved from http://www.nea.org/assets/docs/HE/2005-06StatusTextandAppendixA.pdf

Plecki, M. L., Elfers, A. M., Loeb, H., Zahir, A., & Knapp, M. S. (2005). *Teacher retention and mobility: A look inside and across districts and schools in Washington State*. Silverdale, WA: Center for Strengthening the Teaching Profession. Retrieved from http://depts.washington.edu/ctpmail/PDFs/TeacherRetention.pdf

About the Author

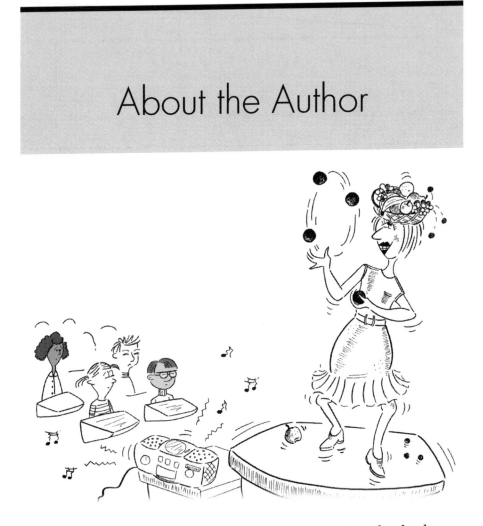

Suzanne Capek Tingley has been a teacher, principal, school super-intendent, and adjunct professor in education administration at the State University of New York at Oswego. She is a writer and consultant for Inside the School (Magna Publications) and her blog, Practical Leadership, is sponsored by the Scholastic Administrator website (http://blogs.scholastic.com/practical_leadership). Her work has appeared in many educational journals including *Education Week*. She received an Outstanding School Administrator Award from the New York State Association of Library Media Specialists and was designated a "Woman of Distinction" by the New York State Senate in 2007.